e.explore

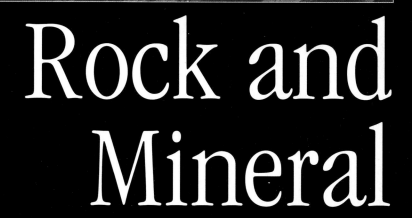

Rock and
Mineral

LONDON, NEW YORK, MELBOURNE,
MUNICH, and DELHI

Project Editor Nigel Ritchie
Weblink Editors Niki Foreman, Roger Brownlie

Project Art Editor Steve Woosnam-Savage
Illustrator Kuo Kang Chen

Senior Editor Clare Lister
Managing Editor Linda Esposito

Managing Art Editor Diane Thistlethwaite

Digital Development Manager Fergus Day
DTP Co-ordinator Tony Cutting

Picture Research Cynthia Frazer
Picture Librarians Kate Ledwith, Sarah Mills, Karl Strange

Jacket Copywriter Adam Powley
Jacket Editor Mariza O'Keeffe

Production Erica Rosen
Jacket Designer Neal Cobourne

Publishing Managers Andrew Macintyre, Caroline Buckingham

Art Director Simon Webb

Consultant Steve Laurie, Sedgwick Museum, Department of Earth
Sciences, University of Cambridge

Produced for DK by Toucan Books Ltd.
Managing Director Ellen Dupont

First published in Great Britain in 2005
by Dorling Kindersley Limited, 80 Strand, London WC2R 0RL

Penguin Group

A CIP catalogue for this book is available from the British Library.

ISBN 1 4053 0365 4

Colour reproduction by Colourscan, Singapore
Printed in China by Toppan Printing Co. (Shenzen) Ltd.

Discover more at
www.dk.com

e.explore

Rock and Mineral

Written by John Farndon

Google

CONTENTS

HOW TO USE THE WEBSITE	6
ROCKY EARTH	8
ROCKS AND MINERALS	10
HISTORY OF GEOLOGY	12
STRUCTURE OF THE EARTH	14
PLATE TECTONICS	16
FORCES OF EROSION	18
THE ROCK CYCLE	20
VOLCANOES	22
IGNEOUS ROCK	24
IDENTIFYING IGNEOUS ROCK	26
METAMORPHIC ROCK	28
REGIONAL METAMORPHISM	30
SEDIMENTARY ROCK	32
CHEMICAL SEDIMENTS	34
CAVES	36
FOSSILS	38
ROCK FROM LIFE-FORMS	40
SPACE ROCK	42
MINERAL CLASSES	44
PHYSICAL PROPERTIES	46
OPTICAL PROPERTIES	48
NATIVE ELEMENTS	50
METAL ELEMENTS	52

GOLD	54
FELSIC SILICATES	56
MAFIC SILICATES	58
QUARTZ	60
OXIDES	62
SULPHIDES	64
SULPHATES AND OTHERS	66
HALIDES	68
CARBONATES AND OTHERS	70
EARLY USES OF MINERALS	72
GEMSTONES	74
DECORATION	76
METALS IN HISTORY	78
MODERN METALS	80
MINERALS IN INDUSTRY	82
MINERALS IN THE HOME	84
MINERALS FOR LIFE	86
GEOLOGY IN THE FIELD	88

REFERENCE SECTION

PROPERTIES	90
GLOSSARY	92
INDEX	94
ACKNOWLEDGEMENTS	96

How to use the e.explore website

e.explore Rock and Mineral has its own website, created by DK and Google™. When you look up a subject in the book, the article gives you key facts and displays a keyword that links you to extra information online. Just follow these easy steps.

http://www.rockandmineral.dke-explore.com

 **1** Enter this website address...

Address : http://www.rockandmineral.dke-explore.com

2 Find the keyword in the book...

sedimentary rock

3 Enter the keyword...

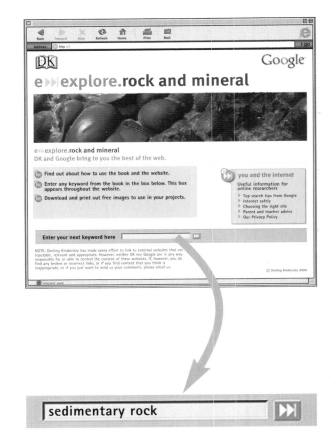

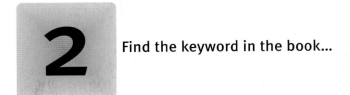
sedimentary rock

You can use only the keywords from the book to search on our website for the specially selected DK/Google links.

Be safe while you are online:

- Always get permission from an adult before connecting to the internet.

- Never give out personal information about yourself.

- Never arrange to meet someone you have talked to online.

- If a site asks you to log in with your name or email address, ask permission from an adult first.

- Do not reply to emails from strangers – tell an adult.

Parents: Dorling Kindersley actively and regularly reviews and updates the links. However, content may change. Dorling Kindersley is not responsible for any site but its own. We recommend that children are supervised while online, that they do not use Chat Rooms, and that filtering software is used to block unsuitable material.

Click on your chosen link...

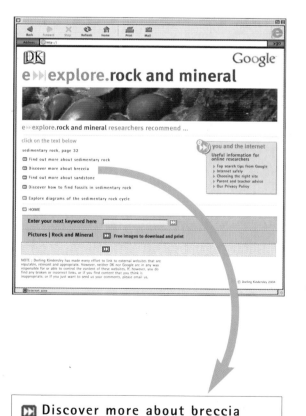

Download fantastic pictures...

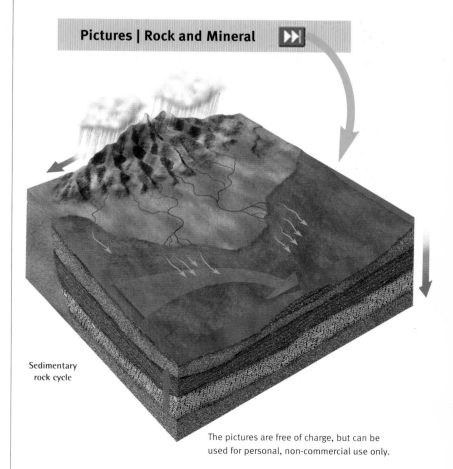

Sedimentary rock cycle

The pictures are free of charge, but can be used for personal, non-commercial use only.

▶▶ Discover more about breccia

Links include animations, videos, sound buttons, virtual tours, interactive quizzes, databases, timelines, and realtime reports.

Go back to the book for your next subject...

UNDERSTANDING THE LANDSCAPE ▲
By studying landscapes, geologists (Earth scientists) can understand the processes that have shaped them over billions of years. The magnificent Grand Canyon (shown above) in Arizona, USA, which is 515 km (320 miles) long, was carved out of the desert by river erosion. This has revealed layers of ancient sandstone, resting on top of granite and gneiss.

Pole for taking lava samples

ROCKY EARTH

Many millions of years ago humans used rocks as the first tools. This stage of humankind's development is known as the Stone Age. Later, people learned to use clay (rock particles) to make pottery, and since then vast numbers of ways of using rocks have been found. Almost every kind of rock can be cut or broken to provide building materials for our homes and cities. A huge range of minerals can be taken from the ground and processed to make particular materials. All our metals, such as iron and steel, come from minerals found in the rock. So too do most of our fuels, such as oil and coal, as well as the salt we put on food, the fertilizers we use to help grow our food, and much more.

◄ VULCANOLOGIST AT WORK
The study of the Earth is such a huge subject that geology is divided into many specialities. Mineralogists study minerals, petrologists study rock, and vulcanologists study volcanoes. Because of the extreme temperatures, vulcanologists often wear special protective clothing, which reflects the heat away from them. Taking lava samples (shown here) for analysis of their mineral content is one method used to monitor volcanic eruptions.

rocks and minerals

MINING AND QUARRYING ►
Rocks and minerals are usually mined or quarried from the ground. Shown here is the Super Pit, Australia's largest opencast goldmine, which is 3 km (2 miles) long. Opencast mining is used when the ore (rocks or minerals from which metal can be extracted for a profit) deposits are close to the surface. It is cheaper and easier than underground mining. Quarries are deep pits dug into the ground to allow the excavation of large quantities of building materials, such as large stone blocks or sand and gravel.

Shuttle body incorporates rare metals such as titanium (from ilmenite)

Fuel tank is made of aluminium (from bauxite)

Inlaid floor made from different coloured marbles

Rocket booster is made mainly from steel, a refined form of iron (from hematite and magnetite)

▲ DECORATIVE ROCKS AND MINERALS

Rocks and minerals can be astonishingly beautiful, especially when carved and polished to make jewels, statues, or the decorative faces of buildings. Few buildings show the beauties of stone better than the Taj Mahal in Agra, India (shown here). Commissioned in 1632 by the Moghul emperor Shah Jahan as a tomb for his beloved wife, it is made from white marble dug from quarries in Rajasthan and inlaid with a wide variety of decorative minerals, such as jade and jasper.

Limey sandstone is all that remains after the white limestone facing was stripped away by looters

▲ BUILT TO LAST

When people want buildings to last, they build from stone because it is so hard-wearing. Few buildings have lasted longer than the Great Pyramids, erected by the Ancient Egyptians more than 3,500 years ago. The Egyptians were experts at using different kinds of rocks, and the pyramids are masterpieces of masonry. The cores of the three Great Pyramids of Giza – two of which are shown here – were made from millions of huge blocks of limey sandstone. These were then covered in brilliant white limestone and finished off with a granite capstone on the summit.

▲ METALS FROM MINERALS

Humans started using metals about 6,500 years ago, taking native metals such as gold and silver from the ground and shaping them into everything from cups to jewellery. In the Middle East, about 4,500 years ago, people discovered that other metals could be extracted from ores by heating them at very high temperatures. With this discovery, a wide range of metals was made available. These provided the raw materials for making nearly all our tools and machinery. Without these metals, technological developments such as the space shuttle (shown here) would never have been possible. All the metals used in the shuttle – from steel and aluminium to rarer light metals such as titanium – come from the Earth's mineral ores.

ROCKS AND MINERALS

Rocks and minerals are the raw materials of the Earth's surface. Rocks are made of countless grains of minerals – some large, some visible only under a microscope. A few rocks are made of a single mineral; others contain half a dozen or more. Minerals are natural, solid chemicals. They are classified according to their chemistry and structure. Rocks are put in three groups according to how they formed: igneous (from molten rock), metamorphic (altered by extreme heat and pressure), and sedimentary (created from layers of sediment – loose material that has settled).

COPPER COMPOUND ▲
Most minerals are compounds (combinations) of at least two chemical elements. Carbonate minerals, for example, form when metals and semi-metals combine with a carbonate, which is a compound of carbon and oxygen. Malachite (shown here) is carbonate formed with copper, which gives it a bright green colour.

Sulphur deposits brought to surface by hot spring activity

Sulphur minerals transported away by river

◄ ELEMENTAL SULPHUR
Only a few minerals are native elements – minerals made entirely from a single chemical element. Even fewer are non-metal native elements. Sulphur is one of these. At the hot springs in Yellowstone Park, USA (shown left), sulphur deposits have been left behind by very hot, mineral-rich water emerging from the Earth's crust.

rocks and minerals

THREE MAIN MINERAL TYPES

NATIVE ELEMENT: METALS
Native metals such as gold (shown here), silver, copper, platinum, and lead are metal elements found in pure form and can be taken straight from a rock or riverbed. But most metals, such as iron, aluminium, and tin, occur in combination with other chemicals. These ores must be processed to extract the metal.

NATIVE ELEMENT: NON-METALS
Sulphur (shown here), graphite, and diamond are the only non-metals found in pure form. Many more non-metal elements are found in combination in minerals. Native sulphur tends to crystallize around hot springs and volcanic craters. However, it is more commonly found in compound sulphide and sulphate minerals.

COMPOSITE MINERALS
Most minerals occur in composite form as compounds of elements, usually when one or more metals combine with a non-metal. These composite minerals are split into nine groups according to which non-metallic combination they contain. Gypsum (shown here) is a sulphate made from calcium, sulphur, and oxygen.

Scree (loose particles) created by weathering of rock on steep mountain slopes

GRANITE MOUNTAIN RANGE ▶
Granite rock forms the backbone of the Sierra Nevada range in California, USA. Granite forms underground when molten magma welling up from the Earth's interior cools and solidifies. It is so tough that it is often exposed at the surface long after softer overlying rock has been weathered away.

Quartz is the main component in granite

Mica biotite comes in a black, plate-like form

Feldspar gives granite a pinkish tint

Soil created by further weathering of rock particles

Granite blocks turned into smooth boulders after prolonged weathering

▲ PHOTOMICROGRAPH OF THIN SLICE OF GRANITE
Most rocks are aggregates – mixtures of minerals. To the naked eye, granite is a light-coloured rock, speckled with black spots. Photographs taken by a polarizing microscope help to distinguish the different minerals present, but the colours appear different from those seen under natural light. Granite is made from three main minerals: black mica, pink or white feldspar, and sandy-grey quartz. Quartz and feldspar minerals form the bulk of many rocks.

THE THREE TYPES OF ROCK

IGNEOUS
Igneous rock begins as magma – rock heated in Earth's interior until it is molten. When magma rises through Earth's crust, it cools and crystallizes into new rock. It can either solidify underground to form intrusive igneous rock such as granite, or erupt on the surface as lava to form extrusive igneous rock, like the basalt shown here.

METAMORPHIC
Metamorphic rock forms when other rocks are transformed by extreme heat or pressure, such as deep volcanic heat or the stresses of mountain building. Sometimes these changes occur locally; sometimes they occur on a vast scale. Some metamorphic rocks, such as gneiss (shown here), take on a banded appearance.

SEDIMENTARY
Sedimentary rock, such as claystone (shown here), forms from sediments – tiny fragments of rock or living matter deposited in layers by wind and water. Older, deeper layers are squeezed under the weight above them and become compacted into solid rock over millions of years in a process known as lithification.

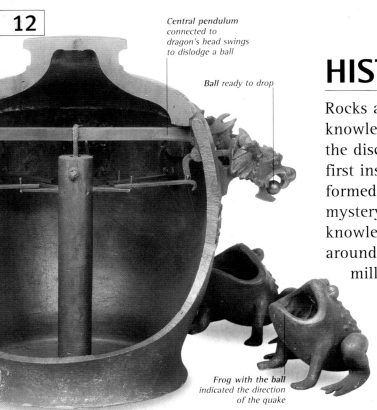

Central pendulum connected to dragon's head swings to dislodge a ball

Ball ready to drop

Frog with the ball indicated the direction of the quake

HISTORY OF GEOLOGY

Rocks and minerals have formed since time began, but our knowledge about them is relatively recent. It was probably the discovery of metals and the search for their ores that first inspired people to find out more about how rocks formed. Yet rocks and minerals remained enough of a mystery to attract many myths. Dramatic advances in our knowledge of the processes that formed the Earth began around 200 years ago with the idea that rocks take millions of years to form.

◄ EARLY EARTHQUAKE DETECTOR
This early geological instrument is a reconstruction of an earthquake detector designed by Chinese scholar Chang Heng about AD 130. It was a heavy urn surrounded by eight dragon heads, each of which held a ball in its mouth. When the earth shook, a ball dropped into the mouth of one of eight frogs around the base, indicating the direction of the quake.

history

▲ MINERALS AND MINING
Much early geological knowledge came from dealing with metal ores. The first great geology book, *De Re Metallica* (*On Metals*), was published in the 16th century by German mining engineer Georgius Agricola. This illustration from it shows miners sifting and washing the mineral ores on a raised channel.

▲ CYCLES OF EROSION
Historians say that modern geology began in the 18th century with the Scottish geologist James Hutton. Hutton argued that the Earth's landscapes were formed and destroyed over millions of years by repeated cycles of erosion, sedimentation, and uplift. The heavily eroded appearance of the mountains of Scotland (shown here) convinced him that these processes were still continuing.

▲ GEOLOGICAL MAPS
Geological maps show where different rock formations occur. The first map (shown here) was made in 1815 by Englishman William Smith as he surveyed routes for canals. He noticed that each rock layer contained its own fossil types. He realized that rocks that formed long distances apart, but which contained the same types of fossils, must be the same age.

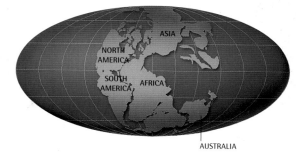

220 MILLION YEARS AGO

AUSTRALIA

100 MILLION YEARS AGO

AUSTRALIA

TODAY

AUSTRALIA

▲ THE PILLARS OF SERAPIS

The influential 19th-century geologist Charles Lyell supported Hutton's theory of continuous geological processes. Crucial to this theory is the idea that whole blocks of land can move up and down over time. On the inside cover of his landmark *Principles of Geology*, Lyell illustrated this with a picture of the 1,600-year-old Temple of Serapis from Pozzuoli on the Italian coast (shown here). Holes, made by shellfish, on the temple columns show that they were once submerged under water before being raised up again.

Markings on the pillars suggest the fall and rise of the land caused by local volcanic and earthquake activity

▲ CONTINENTAL DRIFT

The idea that the Earth's continents moved was first proposed in the 1920s by German meteorologist Alfred Wegener. Wegener pointed to the remarkable match between the east coast of South America and the west coast of Africa and suggested that they had once been joined together. At the time he was ridiculed, but further evidence has proved that the continents are indeed drifting fragments of a former supercontinent.

MINERAL MYTHS

PELE'S HAIR
Volcanoes have inspired many myths. According to Hawaiian legend, the fire-goddess Pele is responsible for their eruptions. Hawaiian lava is very runny. Lava spray flying through the air can stretch into fine, golden-brown fibres of basalt glass. These collect together into the wiry rock known as "Pele's hair" (shown above).

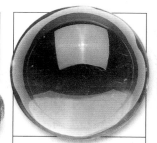

QUARTZ CRYSTAL BALL
Quartz has been valued by many cultures throughout history for its mystical properties. For centuries, people thought that quartz (rock crystal) was ice that had frozen so hard it could not melt. Tibetan monks, Celtic druids, and gypsy psychics have all gazed into "crystal" balls, hoping to see the future.

PROTECTIVE GEMSTONES
The Bible describes a gem-encrusted breastplate (shown here) worn by Aaron, the first High Priest of Israel. Each stone represents one of the 12 Tribes of Israel. The symbolic association of gemstones with people continues today with birthstones. Different gems represent different months of the year.

COPPER SHIELD
Copper was one of the first metals to be used because it is found in the ground in its pure form. Its rarity gave it a high value for trading. These engraved, shield-shaped plaques, known as "coppers", were highly prized as symbols of wealth and prosperity by Native American Northwest Coast tribes.

AMULET
Ancient Egyptians used jewelled amulets (charms) to protect them from harm. Some precious and semi-precious stones, such as turquoise, were believed to possess magical powers. This scarab (sacred dung beetle) was used as a chest amulet. It is shown supporting a red carnelian, which symbolizes the Sun.

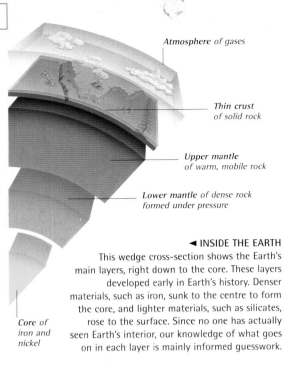

Atmosphere of gases

Thin crust
of solid rock

Upper mantle
of warm, mobile rock

Lower mantle of dense rock
formed under pressure

Core of
iron and
nickel

◀ INSIDE THE EARTH
This wedge cross-section shows the Earth's main layers, right down to the core. These layers developed early in Earth's history. Denser materials, such as iron, sunk to the centre to form the core, and lighter materials, such as silicates, rose to the surface. Since no one has actually seen Earth's interior, our knowledge of what goes on in each layer is mainly informed guesswork.

LAYERS OF THE EARTH

CRUST
The crust (0–40 km, 0–25 miles) is Earth's thin, upper layer. It is made up of mostly silicate-rich rocks, such as basalt (shown here). It is attached in giant slabs to the hard part of the upper mantle to form the lithosphere. These slabs drift on the mantle below causing continental drift, volcanoes, and earthquakes.

UPPER MANTLE
The rigid lithosphere floats on a layer of the upper mantle (16–670 km, 10–420 miles) known as the asthenosphere. Rock here is so hot that it melts in places to form magma that sometimes erupts on the surface through volcanoes. Upper mantle rock, such as peridotite (shown here), is denser than crustal rock.

LOWER MANTLE
In the lower mantle (670–2,900 km, 420–1,800 miles), huge pressures turn the lighter, silicate minerals of the upper mantle into very dense pyroxene (shown here) and perovskite minerals. Perovskite is the most abundant mineral in the mantle and therefore the Earth, since the mantle makes up 80 per cent of the Earth's volume.

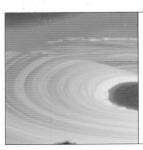

CORE
The Earth's core (2,900–6,370 km, 1,800–3,960 miles) is a dense ball of mostly iron with some nickel. The outer core is so hot, reaching temperatures of more than 3,300°C (6,000°F) that the metal is molten. The inner core is even hotter, reaching 7,000°C (12,600°F), but enormous pressures prevent the iron from melting.

STRUCTURE OF THE EARTH

The deepest boreholes dug by geologists only penetrate 15 km (9 miles) into the Earth. But geologists have found out about the different layers of the Earth's interior by analysing earthquake waves. The surface is a thin, rocky crust, barely 6 km (4 miles) thick in places. Below this, a very thick mantle of rock flows like sticky treacle. A further 2,900 km (1,800 miles) down is a core of iron and nickel – with a centre under so much pressure it cannot melt, despite temperatures of 7,000°C (12,600°F).

EXPOSED PERIDOTITE FROM THE UPPER MANTLE

Geologists can only study directly rocks that are on the Earth's surface. However, rocks from deep in the mantle are occasionally brought to the surface by tectonic plate movement and volcanic activity. This photograph shows a massive slab of weathered peridotite from the Tablelands of Gros Morne in Newfoundland, Canada. In this case, immense forces have shoved a slab of oceanic plate (combining the crust with the upper layer of the upper mantle) onto the continental plate, exposing dense peridotite rock from the mantle.

▼ CUTTING THROUGH THE CRUST
This diagram shows a cross-section of the Earth's crust and lithosphere with some of the main features of the landscape – and how these surface features relate to what is going on below them in Earth's interior. Notice how ridges on the ocean floor align with cracks in the crust where hot material from the mantle rises up. Notice too how volcanoes erupt over weak points in the crust or plate boundaries. Changes in pressure created by the movement of plates help to melt the mantle material and cause it to erupt.

Lithosphere extends about 100 km (60 miles) below the surface

Old mountains mark the edge of a stable slab of lithosphere

Mountain ranges are made from layers of rock crumpled by plate movements

AURORA BOREALIS (NORTHERN LIGHTS) ►

This spectacular light show, seen in the sky above the North Pole, is known as the aurora borealis. A similar phenomenon above the South Pole is known as the aurora australis. Both are caused when electrically charged particles pouring from the Sun are drawn into the atmosphere by Earth's magnetic field and flung towards the Earth. These then collide with air particles, making the upper air glow around the poles. Scientists believe the Earth's magnetic field or magnetosphere, which extends far out into space, is generated deep inside our planet by the rotating liquid outer core.

▲ MAGNETIC ROCK

Some minerals found on Earth, such as magnetite (shown here) and pyrrhotite, are naturally magnetic. When these minerals move freely in molten magma, they line up with the Earth's magnetic field. The alignment of such minerals in old rocks can reveal a great deal about the movement of the continents.

Earth's structure

MINERALS THAT MAKE UP THE EARTH

IRON
Most of the Earth's minerals are made from four chemical elements – iron (35%), oxygen (28%), magnesium (17%), and silicon (13%). Although iron makes up a third of the Earth's weight and most of the core, it is rarely found in the crust as a pure element. It is usually joined with other elements in compounds.

SILICON
Much of Earth's crust is made from combinations of two elements – oxygen and silicon – called silicates. These materials are so light that they rose to form the crust early in the Earth's history. Silicon is rarely found on its own, but is almost always found joined to oxygen as a silicate. Quartz is a typical silicate mineral.

MAGNESIUM
Magnesium is the third most common element in the Earth. Silicates containing iron and magnesium are the most common minerals found in the upper mantle. Lower mantle minerals are mostly magnesium compounds attached to iron and oxygen. Magnesium is also found in many silicates in the crust.

NICKEL
Nickel is quite a rare element in Earth's crust, appearing as nickel-iron or in compounds. Much of the Earth's core is made from nickel-iron. Iron meteorites falling to Earth are rich in nickel-iron, showing that nickel was a key element in the early Solar System. Nickel for industry is extracted from the ore pentlandite.

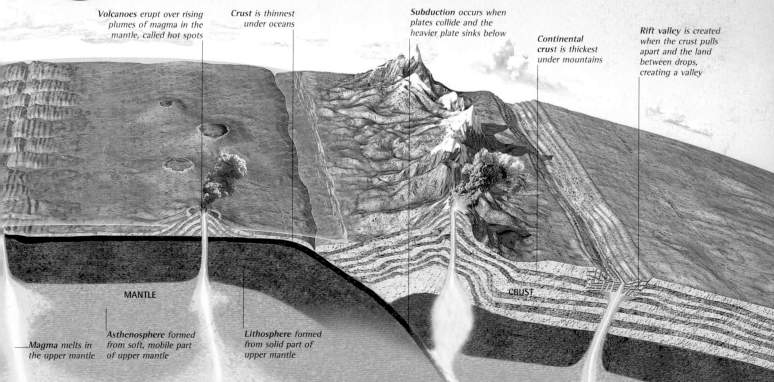

Volcanoes erupt over rising plumes of magma in the mantle, called hot spots

Crust is thinnest under oceans

Subduction occurs when plates collide and the heavier plate sinks below

Continental crust is thickest under mountains

Rift valley is created when the crust pulls apart and the land between drops, creating a valley

MANTLE

CRUST

Magma melts in the upper mantle

Asthenosphere formed from soft, mobile part of upper mantle

Lithosphere formed from solid part of upper mantle

PLATE TECTONICS

The Earth's continents have not always been where they are now. In fact, they are moving around very slowly beneath our feet all the time. It is not just the continents that are moving – so is the ocean floor. Earth's rigid outer shell of rock (made up of the crust and the hard, upper part of the mantle) is split into 20 or so giant slabs known as tectonic plates – seven huge ones and about a dozen smaller ones – which are jostling one another all the time. The continents are embedded in these plates and so move with them.

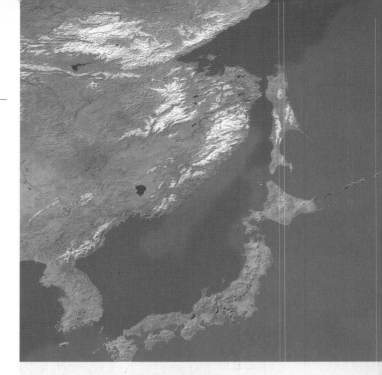

▲ CONVERGING: OCEAN TO OCEAN

In some places, tectonic plates are converging (colliding). The denser plate (usually oceanic) sinks, while the lighter one rides over it, forcing it down into the mantle. This is called subduction. Melted material from the subducted plate forces its way up through the weakened edge of the overlying plate to create a string of volcanoes. When the overlying plate is oceanic, the effect creates an arc of volcanic islands. The islands of Japan were created in this way – the Pacific and Philippine plates were subducted beneath the North American and Eurasian plates.

PLATE BOUNDARIES

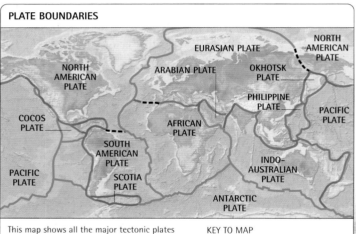

NORTH AMERICAN PLATE
EURASIAN PLATE
NORTH AMERICAN PLATE
ARABIAN PLATE
OKHOTSK PLATE
PHILIPPINE PLATE
PACIFIC PLATE
COCOS PLATE
AFRICAN PLATE
SOUTH AMERICAN PLATE
INDO-AUSTRALIAN PLATE
PACIFIC PLATE
SCOTIA PLATE
ANTARCTIC PLATE

This map shows all the major tectonic plates and some of the smaller ones. The plates move together in three ways: pushing together (convergent), moving apart (divergent), or sliding past (transform). Of the seven large plates – the Pacific, African, North and South American, Eurasian, Indo-Australian, and Antarctic – only the Pacific does not carry a continent. Plates under oceans are the newest, since they are always forming at divergent boundaries.

KEY TO MAP
—————— convergent boundary
—————— divergent boundary
—————— transform fault
- - - - - uncertain boundary

DIVERGING BOUNDARY ▶

In some places – usually mid-ocean – tectonic plates are slowly diverging (moving apart). As they separate, molten magma from the Earth's interior wells up through the gap and solidifies creating new crust. In this way, the seabed spreads wider and wider. The Atlantic Ocean is growing by about 20 cm (8 in) every year. The upwelling of hot magma from the Earth's mantle along the crack where the plates are pulling apart, creates a long, raised ridge along the ocean floor. This is known as the mid-ocean ridge. Thingvellir in Iceland is one of the few places where this ridge can be seen on the land.

plate tectonics

Eurasian plate is pulling eastwards away from the North American plate

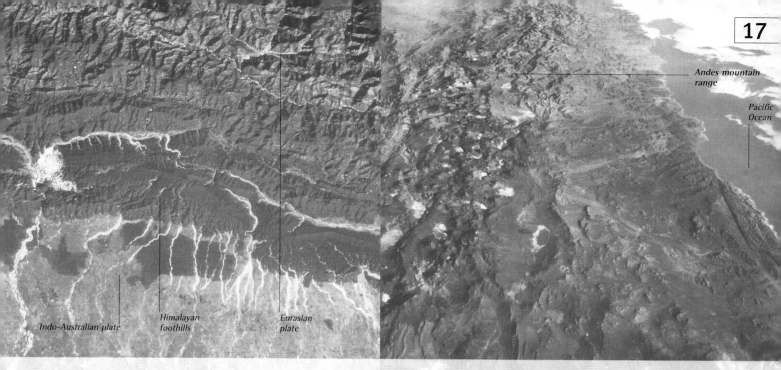

Indo-Australian plate   Himalayan foothills   Eurasian plate

Andes mountain range

Pacific Ocean

▲ CONVERGING: CONTINENT TO CONTINENT

Sometimes two plates carrying continental landmasses collide. This is what is happening in southern Asia where the Indo-Australian plate is driving northwards into the Eurasian plate. The tremendous power of this collision has distorted the rocks of both continents. Here, the Himalayas – the world's highest mountains – have been thrown up like a great wave as India ploughs into Asia. India is still moving northwards by nearly 5 cm (2 in) every year. The mountains spread out far and wide from the line of impact.

▲ CONVERGING: OCEAN TO CONTINENT

Where an oceanic plate is subducted beneath another plate, there is often a very deep trench in the ocean floor. All around the Pacific, plates are being subducted. Some of the world's deepest trenches, such as the Mariana trench, which is 10,920 m (35,830 ft) deep, mark the point where these plates descend into the mantle. The collision of the Nazca plate with the South American plate has not only created a deep ocean trench, but has also crumpled up the western edge of the continent to create the world's longest mountain range, the Andes.

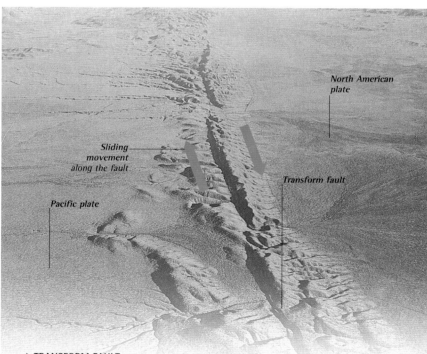

North American plate

Sliding movement along the fault

Transform fault

Pacific plate

▲ TRANSFORM FAULT

The relentless movement of the Earth's tectonic plates can put the rock under so much strain that it fractures. This creates a crack in the Earth called a fault. Where this fault marks a boundary between two tectonic plates, it is known as a transform fault. The San Andreas fault (shown here) in California, USA, is the world's most famous transform fault. East of the fault lies the North American plate. To its west lies the Pacific plate, which is slowly rotating anticlockwise. As it rotates, the Pacific plate slides along the fault – generating the earthquakes that are common in the region.

TYPES OF FAULT

NORMAL FAULT
Areas or zones of fault activity tend to be near plate margins. A normal fault occurs where two tectonic plates are diverging. The resulting tension pulls blocks of rock apart, allowing one block to slip down. The surface that it slips down is called the fault plane. Huge cliffs, known as fault scarps, can be created this way.

REVERSE OR THRUST
Where tectonic plates coverge, the force of collision can compress (squeeze) the rocks so much that it creates reverse faults. This is where one block of rock is pushed up and over another. If the fault is very shallow – so that it is almost horizontal – it is called a thrust fault. Landslides are often associated with these faults.

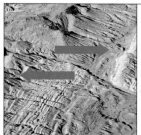

STRIKE-SLIP
Sometimes, plates neither converge nor diverge. Instead they slide past each other horizontally. In this case, they tear blocks of rock apart sideways, creating a strike-slip fault like this one in Nevada in the USA. Transform faults between plates, such as the San Andreas fault, are gigantic strike-slip faults.

FORCES OF EROSION

Mountains, hills, valleys, and plains look as if they have been in place forever. But all Earth's landscapes are being worn away slowly by the weather, by running water, moving ice, waves, wind, and natural chemicals. Occasionally, the effect is sudden and dramatic – as when an entire hillside is washed away in a heavy rainstorm. But most of the time the weathering is so slow that you barely notice it. Over tens of thousands of years, mountains crumble, hills are worn flat, and valleys are broadened into plains. The process of breaking up rock and carrying off the fragments is called erosion. Deposition happens when material picked up by water, wind or ice, is dropped again.

erosion

Avalanches feed the glacier with ice and rock debris

Arches created by wind erosion

◄ WEATHERING

Wherever rock is exposed to air, wind, sun, and rain, it starts to break down in a process called weathering. Over time, weathering can break up the hardest granite eventually turning it to sand. Sometimes rock can be broken by changes in the weather, such as extreme heat and cold. For example, water freezing in cracks can expand with such force that it shatters solid rock. Repeated cycles of freezing and thawing help to erode exposed mountain peaks.

◄ CORROSION

Sometimes rocks are attacked by chemicals in the air or dissolved in rainwater. In limestone country, the effects of chemical corrosion are very visible. Carbon dioxide in the air dissolves in rainwater to form carbonic acid. The acid is weak, but as the rainwater trickles down through cracks in the rock, it eats away the limestone very quickly. Cracks in a limestone plateau are often etched into deep grooves called grykes, like those shown here.

Glacier moves slowly along the valley floor

Stripes on the glacier show the debris being carried along

◄ WATER EROSION

Water is a powerful agent of erosion. Inland rivers carve out deep valleys as they run down to the sea. Coastal waves, packed full of energy by wind blowing over huge expanses of ocean, batter the shore relentlessly. As well as pounding the coastal rock with wave-borne shingle, they also split the rock apart by ramming air into the cracks. Sometimes the constant battering of the waves undercuts coastal slopes to create cliffs. These cliffs may then be further undermined, making them collapse. This can leave lonely stacks like the Twelve Apostles (shown here) on Australia's Victoria coast.

◄ GLACIAL EROSION

On some mountains it is so cold that snow never melts and over the years slowly compacts into a mass of ice. Eventually, this mass becomes so heavy that it starts to flow slowly downhill, forming a river of ice called a glacier. Today, glaciers such as the Batura Glacier in Gojal, Pakistan, (shown here) form only in the highest mountains and in the polar regions. But in the past, during the long, cold periods called Ice Ages, vast areas of North America and Europe were buried under ice. The sheer weight of glaciers gives them the power to shape the landscape. They gouge out huge, U-shaped valleys, scoop deep bowls called cirques, remove entire hills, and push frost-shattered rock debris into massive piles known as moraines.

◄ WIND EROSION

In damp regions the power of the wind plays little part in shaping the land. But in dry landscapes, such as deserts, the wind can blast suspended dust and sand at rocks with devastating effect. Sometimes the abrasive action of the sand (which acts like very rough sandpaper) can sculpt the rock into fantastic shapes, like this sandstone Turret Arch from the Arches National Park in Utah, USA. Wind can also roll loose rocks and sand along the desert floor, scooping out shallow bowls called blowouts. Geologists once thought that deserts were shaped mostly by the wind, but the effect of floods in the past may be even more important.

▲ TRANSPORTATION

As rock is worn away, the fragments are transported or carried away by water, ice, or – if the debris is fine and dry – blown away by the wind. The material carried along by a river is called its load. It varies according to the speed and volume of water in the river and the kind of terrain it is flowing through. Some rivers, like China's Huang He and the Amazon in South America (shown here), carry so much silt at certain times of the year that they turn brown or yellow.

TYPES OF DEPOSITION

DELTA
As a river flows into the sea or a lake, it slows down and can no longer carry its load of silt. Often, the silt is dumped over a fan-shaped area called a delta, where the river splits into smaller branches called distributaries. This aerial view shows mud being deposited in a delta off the east coast of New Caledonia.

FLOODPLAIN
As a river nears the sea, it becomes shallower and meanders across broad valleys. When the river floods, it leaves behind a wide floodplain of fine sand and mud. This view of the River Nile in Egypt clearly shows the extent of these deposits. Annual flooding has created a rich, fertile corridor of land in the midst of the desert.

DESERT DUNES
In some deserts, the wind piles up vast seas of sand into giant dunes. In the Sahara Desert of northern Africa, these dunes can grow up to 100 km (60 miles) long and rise up to 200 m (650 ft) high. They form a dramatic, ever-changing landscape depending on the amount of sand and the strength and direction of the wind.

LOESS
Wind action is not just important in deserts, but wherever there is light, loose material – such as on a beach and at a glacier's edge. These eroded peaks in Iowa, USA, were formed by wind-blown silt, called loess, left behind by retreating glaciers during the last Ice Age. Vast areas of Central Asia are also covered by loess deposits.

THE ROCK CYCLE

Erosion relentlessly destroys rock wherever it is exposed on the Earth's surface, but new rocks are always being made from the remants of the old ones. This recycling is called the rock cycle. Some parts are quick and obvious – cliffs crumble and volcanoes bring up lava. Much of the cycle, however is hidden deep in the Earth and happens over millions of years. Plate movements turn sedimentary and igneous rocks into metamorphic rocks, or turn metamorphic rocks into igneous rocks.

A ROCK JOURNEY

EROSION
Even these tough-looking basalt cliffs will be broken down in the perpetual rock cycle. In time, they will be worn to sand by pounding waves. The sand may form new sediments, or it may be subducted into the mantle along with the seabed and mix with rising magma to form new igneous rock.

FROST-SHATTERING
The rock cycle can happen anywhere. These igneous rocks scattered across a Welsh hillside in the UK have been shattered by water seeping into cracks and expanding as it freezes. When further erosion has made the fragments small enough, they will be carried away down the hillside by water, wind, or ice.

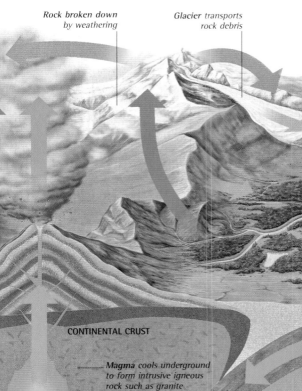

Sulphur and carbon gases from volcanoes contribute to chemical weathering

Rock broken down by weathering

Glacier transports rock debris

Sediments deposited in layers eventually turn to rock

SEDIMENTARY ROCK

Molten lava cools on the surface to form extrusive igneous rock such as basalt

CONTINENTAL CRUST

Magma cools underground to form intrusive igneous rock such as granite

METAMORPHIC ROCK

Rising magma fills chamber in the crust

Sediments and oceanic crust are subducted beneath another plate

IGNEOUS ROCK

IGNEOUS ROCK

Sediments and crust on subducting plate melts, creating magma

▲ **DUST CLOUD OVER JAPAN**
Even the wind can play its part in the rock cycle. In this photograph, fine dust blown off the plains of Central Asia is carried eastwards over the Sea of Japan. Eventually, the dust will settle and sink to the seabed where it may form new sedimentary rock or be carried back into the mantle by subduction (the downward movement of one plate beneath another).

THE ROCK CYCLE ▶
This diagram shows how the Earth's rocks are continually being made, destroyed, and remade in the rock cycle. Material brought to the crust as magma (molten rock) in intrusions and volcanoes forms igneous rock. Exposed on the Earth's surface, the rocks are eroded, and the fragments may be washed into the sea where they solidify into new sedimentary rock. This rock may then be uplifted to form mountains or tranformed by heat and pressure into metamorphic rock. Sedimentary and metamorphic rock can also be exposed and eroded. The fragments may be washed into the sea to form new sedimentary rock, or be carried down into the mantle by subduction to eventually rise again as magma or be transformed into metamorphic rock.

TRANSPORTATION
To form new rock, weathered fragments must be carried to places where they can accumulate. Here a river can be seen depositing sediment (the lighter patches) on its bed on every twist and turn of its course. When these sediments turn to rock, the ripple marks of the river may be clearly visible.

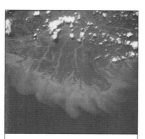

DEPOSITION
Some sediments are washed all the way down a river to the sea where they are deposited in a delta, such as this one off southeast Borneo, Indonesia. Heavier grains are dropped first and tend to compact into sandstone. Lighter sediments are carried further out and settle to form shale and mudstone.

SEDIMENTARY ROCK
Once sediments have lithified (turned to rock), the beds may be raised to the surface by the movement of tectonic plates. There exposed rocks, like the shale beds shown here, can be eroded by water and weather to provide raw material for new rock. Unexposed sedimentary rock may be metamorphosed into new rock.

METAMORPHIC ROCK
All kinds of rock – igneous, metamorphic, or sedimentary – can be altered by heat and pressure to form new metamorphic rock. For example, shale changes into slate when subjected to tectonic pressure. Slate can then be altered by more extreme heat and pressures to form schist (shown here) and gneiss.

IGNEOUS ROCK
Lava erupting on the surface or magma solidifying underground constantly refill the Earth's crust with new rock. Yet even this material is recycled. The lava erupting here off the coast of Hawaii may contain material that was subducted millions of years ago, and which has since circulated through the mantle.

Sediments washed out to sea, deposited in layers, and lithified

◄ ERRATIC BOULDER
These giant boulders, known as erratics, are rolled over the landscape by glaciers. Some have been carried up to 800 km (500 miles) before the glacier melts and leaves them behind. They may look too large to be part of the rock cycle, but even the biggest boulders are eventually reduced to sedimentary rock-forming sand and clay by prolonged weathering.

Magma forms mid-ocean ridge, where plates are pulling apart

MID-OCEAN RIDGE

rock cycle

Sediments carried out to the deep ocean floor

OCEANIC CRUST

LITHOSPHERE

Magma wells up between diverging plates

THE PROCESSES IN THE ROCK CYCLE

Diverging and converging tectonic plates create new igneous rock. Subduction often triggers volcanic activity and upwelling of magma

Weathering by wind, rain, and chemicals, such as sulphuric acid from volcanic eruptions, breaks down exposed rock

Rock fragments are transported by water (rain, rivers, sea), wind, and ice (glaciers)

Rock fragments are deposited as sediments on the land and seabed where they are compressed and compacted into rock

Rock is uplifted and exposed at the surface by plate movements

Exposure to pressure (from mountain-building) and heat (from magma) alters existing rock to create new metamorphic rock

MAGMA

ASTHENOSPHERE

▲ PILLOW LAVA ON THE MID-ATLANTIC RIDGE
Running right down the middle of the Atlantic Ocean is a crack between two major tectonic plates. These plates are slowly moving apart, allowing lava to ooze up through the gap and cool on the receding edges, forming a raised mid-ocean ridge. The hot lava solidifies in pillow-shaped lumps, called pillow lava, as it rapidly cools in the cold sea water.

VOLCANOES

At certain places on the Earth, hot magma emerges onto the surface from deep underground, flowing out over the ground as red-hot lava. These places are known as volcanoes. Sometimes, a volcano can become clogged up with a thick plug of magma – then it suddenly erupts in a gigantic explosion, throwing out jets of steam and fiery fragments high into the air. Successive eruptions can build up such a huge cone of ash and lava around the volcano that it becomes a mountain.

◄ STROMBOLIAN ERUPTION
In places where the magma is acidic and sticky – typically along converging plate margins – volcanic eruptions are often quite dramatic, as on Mount Etna, Sicily (shown here). When Etna erupts, it repeatedly spits out blobs of lava. This is called a Strombolian eruption, after Stromboli, an island off Sicily.

Blobs of molten magma

Huge clouds of ash and steam

GLOBAL VOLCANIC ACTIVITY

Volcanoes are places where magma (molten rock) breaks through to the surface and are not randomly located. All but a few of the world's active volcanoes lie close to the margins of tectonic plates, especially in a ring around the Pacific Ocean known as the "Ring of Fire". The exceptions are hot-spot volcanoes, such as Mauna Loa, Hawaii, which was formed as the Pacific plate moved over a fixed hot spot. It is a shield volcano with frequent but gentle eruptions.

TYPES OF VOLCANO

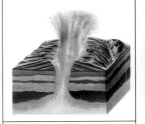

STRATOVOLCANO
When sticky magma erupts explosively from a single vent, successive eruptions build up a distinctive cone-shaped mountain from layers of lava and ash. The characteristic steep shape is due to the sticky lava cooling and hardening before it can spread very far. Stratovolcanoes are also known as composite volcanoes.

SHIELD
Where tectonic plates are pulling apart, magma reaches the surface easily, so it is less acidic and less sticky. Runny basalt lava floods out steadily to form broad, gently sloping volcanoes – often more than 10 km (6 miles) wide – known as shield volcanoes. Mauna Loa on Hawaii is the world's largest shield volcano.

FISSURE
Not all eruptions come from a single hole; fissure eruptions occur where lava floods up to the surface through a long crack. Large-scale fissures mainly occur along mid-ocean ridges, where tectonic plates are pulling apart. Small fissures occur on the flanks of large volcanoes, creating a "curtain of fire" as the lava spurts up.

TYPES OF EFFUSIVE LAVA

PAHOEHOE
Effusive volcanoes produce two very distinctive kinds of lava, known by their Hawaiian names of pahoehoe and a'a. Pahoehoe is common in Hawaiian eruptions. This very fluid lava flows rapidly over large areas. As its surface cools, it wrinkles into rope-like coils, while molten lava continues to flow beneath it.

A'A
Hawaiian volcanoes are famous for their spectacular jet-like sprays of lava called fire fountains. This lava cools and clots as it falls, creating a lumpy lava called a'a (pronounced "ah-ah"), which is slower-flowing than pahoehoe. As a'a piles up on the ground, a thick skin forms, which crumbles as it oozes forwards.

volcanoes

▲ RIVER OF LAVA FROM MOUNT ETNA, SICILY
Lava is the name given to molten magma after it has emerged onto the surface. Explosive volcanoes tend to produce lava and other debris in short spurts during eruptions. By contrast, effusive (flowing) volcanoes ooze lava almost continuously. Mount Etna, which displays a complex mixture of stratovolcano and shield volcano characteristics, is a continuously active volcano that produces mainly effusive lava and mild explosive eruptions.

Ash and steam blasted high into the air

▲ PLINIAN ERUPTION
Plinian eruptions, such as this one seen on Mount St Helens, USA in 1980, are the most explosive of all. They are named after Pliny the Younger. He witnessed the devastating eruption of Mount Vesuvius, which buried the Roman city of Pompeii in AD 79. In eruptions such as these, an explosion of steam and carbon dioxide gas blasts clouds of burning ash and volcanic fragments high into the stratosphere.

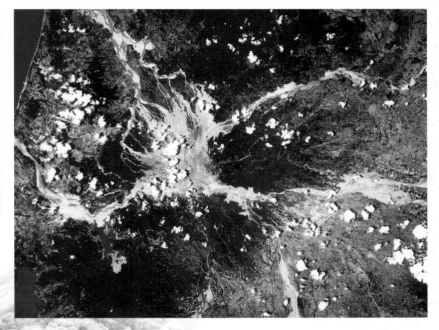

▲ MUDFLOWS ON MOUNT PINATUBO
The eruption of Mount Pinatubo in the Philippines in June 1991 was one of the largest of the twentieth century. However, the main devastation came not from the initial explosion, nor from hot lava, but from deadly mudflows of rain mixed with ash and rock debris that covered the land (as seen on this satellite photo), destroying crops and causing thousands of buildings to collapse.

Pyroclastic cloud of ash and magma moves very fast

◄ PYROCLASTIC FLOW, MOUNT PINATUBO
Often the most devastating effects of an eruption like that of Mount Pinatubo come from pyroclastic flows, or *nuées ardentes* (glowing clouds). These are scorching avalanches of ash and pyroclasts – chunks of solid magma shattered by the explosion – that roar down the side of a volcano. These flows can reach speeds of 500 kmh (300 mph) and temperatures of up to 800°C (1,470°F), incinerating everything in their path.

IGNEOUS ROCK

Although often covered by a thin layer of sedimentary rock, igneous rock forms most of the Earth's crust. There are more than 600 different kinds, but all form from magma – molten rock from Earth's hot interior. This cools and crystallizes as it nears the surface into solid masses of hard rock. Sometimes the magma erupts from volcanoes before it turns to rock. Rock like this is described as volcanic or extrusive igneous rock. Sometimes the rock forms intrusively, when magma solidifies underground to form structures, such as batholiths, dykes, and sills.

ROCK FORMATION IN ACTION ▶
At some volcanoes, like these in Hawaii, it is possible to see igneous rock actually being formed. The hot magma oozes onto the surface as lava and flows out across the landscape. The lava's surface cools so quickly that it forms a crust of rock, while red-hot lava flows on below. Lava cools so quickly that there is no time for crystals to grow. This results in very fine-grained volcanic rocks such as basalt.

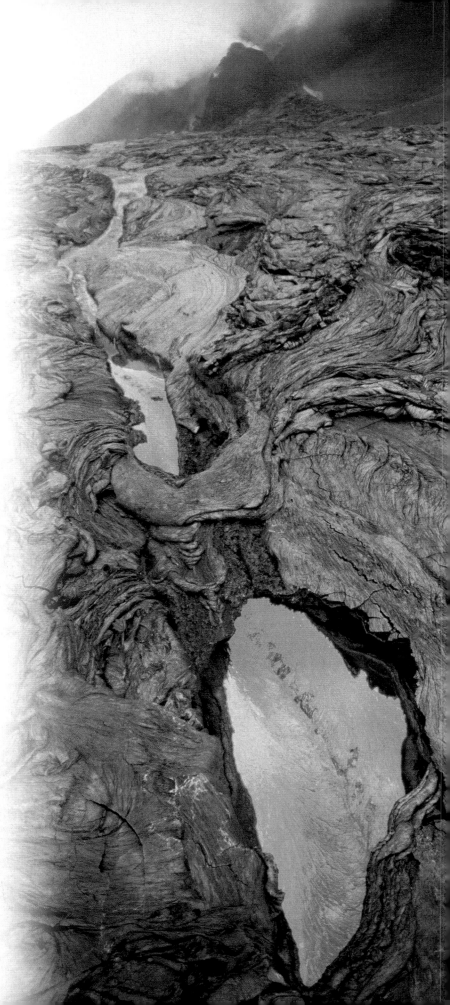

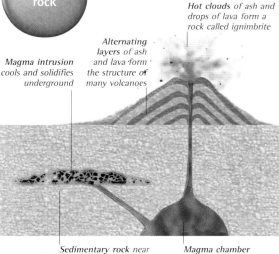

Hot clouds of ash and drops of lava form a rock called ignimbrite

Alternating layers of ash and lava form the structure of many volcanoes

Magma intrusion cools and solidifies underground

Sedimentary rock near an intrusion may melt

Magma chamber supplies huge volumes of hot magma

▲ MAGMA INTO ROCK
Magma can form igneous rock either by erupting on the surface through volcanoes, or by solidifying in masses underground. Volcanoes spew out magma in many different forms – as molten rock (lava), as ash, as cinders, or even as froth – all of which can cool and turn to rock. Volcanic ash, for example, forms a rock called tuff. The froth on top of molten lava forms pumice, a rock so light and full of holes that it can float.

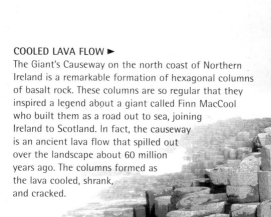

COOLED LAVA FLOW ►

The Giant's Causeway on the north coast of Northern Ireland is a remarkable formation of hexagonal columns of basalt rock. These columns are so regular that they inspired a legend about a giant called Finn MacCool who built them as a road out to sea, joining Ireland to Scotland. In fact, the causeway is an ancient lava flow that spilled out over the landscape about 60 million years ago. The columns formed as the lava cooled, shrank, and cracked.

Basalt pillar forms a natural paving stone

INTRUSIVE STRUCTURES

BATHOLITH
Immense bubbles of hot magma can force their way up towards the Earth's surface, pushing other rock aside, or melting it. Some bubbles harden below the surface, creating giant masses of hard rock called batholiths. Over millions of years, the soft rock surrounding them erodes, turning the exposed batholiths into mountains.

DYKE
A dyke on the landscape shows where upwelling magma split the overlying rock and forced itself up through the crack. As the softer overlying rock is worn away, the wall or dyke is left standing proud above the landscape. Dykes and other intrusions that cut across existing rock structures are called discordant intrusions.

SILL
The dark band of rock visible here is a sill, a thin band of igneous rock that forms when hot magma oozes its way into a crack between two layers of rock. This can sometimes leave a thin strip of igneous rock across a wide area. Sills and other intrusions that follow existing rock structures are called concordant intrusions.

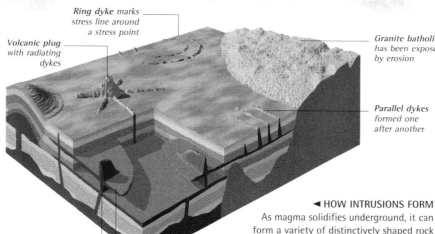

Ring dyke marks stress line around a stress point

Volcanic plug with radiating dykes

Granite batholith has been exposed by erosion

Parallel dykes formed one after another

Vertical dyke follows stress lines through strata

Horizontal sill intrudes between layers of rock

◄ HOW INTRUSIONS FORM
As magma solidifies underground, it can form a variety of distinctively shaped rock formations. Typically, it forms large domes (batholiths) as the magma bubbles up through the ground, or thin sheets in cracks called dykes and sills. But magma intrusions can also take on other shapes, depending on the pressure of the magma and the existing rock structure.

COARSE-GRAINED PEGMATITE ►
The crystals in this pegmatite rock are so large that they are easy to see without a microscope. Large crystals indicate that the rock cooled slowly in an intrusion deep underground. Pegmatites typically form in fissures (cracks) that open up when granite batholiths cool and solidify. They are basically granite but can contain giant crystals of gems such as topaz and beryl. The dark crystals seen here are tourmaline.

Tourmaline crystal took time to grow this large

FINE-GRAINED ANDESITE ►
Andesites are the most common volcanic rocks after basalt. They get their name from the Andes mountains in South America. Andesite is formed from a sticky lava that tends to clog up volcanoes before bursting through in a mighty explosion. Like most volcanic rocks, andesite is fine-grained because it cools rapidly on the Earth's surface. However, this sample includes larger crystals that formed in the magma before it reached the surface.

IDENTIFYING IGNEOUS ROCK

All igneous rocks are crystalline (made of crystals joined together). It is usually easy to recognize them by their shiny, grainy appearance. A few, such as obsidian, have a glassy (no grain) appearance. The chemical composition of the magma, where it formed (above or below the ground), and how quickly it cooled, all contribute to the formation of different igneous rocks. Acid magmas form pale rocks like rhyolite; less acid magmas form darker rocks like basalt. Rocks that form deep down, such as granite, are coarse-grained because they cool slowly. Rocks that form near the surface, such as basalt, are fine-grained because they cool quickly.

▲ OBSIDIAN BLADE
Obsidian is a jet-black, glassy rock, prized by the Central American Aztecs, who used it to make sacrificial knives (shown here). It forms when rhyolitic lava cools so quickly that there is no time for crystals to form. Obsidian is usually only found where there has been recent volcanic activity. It tends to go dull and sugary over hundreds of years.

GRAIN SIZE (RATE OF COOLING)

FINE-GRAIN (FAST)
Lava tends to cool too quickly for large crystals to grow much and so produces rocks that are fine-grained. The crystals are too small to identify with the naked eye, but they can be seen twinkling if the rock is turned in the light. The three most common fine-grained rocks are basalt, andesite, and rhyolite (shown here).

MEDIUM-GRAIN (MEDIUM)
Magma that cools more slowly in underground dykes and sills forms medium-sized grains. These are large enough to see, but not to identify with the naked eye. Dolerite (shown here) is the most common form of medium-grained rock, forming both the Palisades Sill in New Jersey, USA, and the Great Whin Sill in England.

COARSE-GRAIN (SLOW)
Magma that crystallizes in large masses deep down cools very slowly. This gives plenty of time for crystals – such as the dark tourmaline and pink feldspar shown in this lump of pegmatite – to grow large enough to see with the naked eye. The most common coarse-grained igneous rocks are granite and gabbro.

◄ PORPHYRY VASE
This beautiful Ancient Egyptian vase from c. 2900 BC is made from porphyry. Porphyries are medium or fine-grained igneous rocks usually containing large crystals of feldspar. Typically, porphyries develop where a magma containing large crystals that have formed deep down is injected into surface rock features such as a dyke or sill.

Famous US presidents carved into Mt Rushmore include George Washington

e▶▶ igneous rock

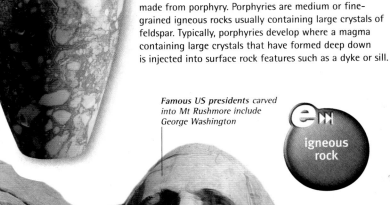

GRANITE-FACED PRESIDENTS ►
Igneous rock is so tough that anything made from it – whether a building or carving – tends to be very long-lasting. The four US presidents' heads (Washington, Jefferson, Theodore Roosevelt, and Lincoln) on Mount Rushmore in the Black Hills of South Dakota, USA, were carved out of 1.7-billion-year-old granite. The work took 14 years. The presidents will probably keep their features for tens of thousands of years. The white streaks on the foreheads of Washington and Lincoln are pegmatite dykes.

CLASSIFICATION BY CHEMICAL COMPOSITION

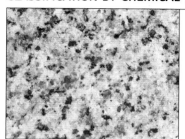

ACID
Magma containing more than 65 per cent silica is said to be acid. Acid rock also has a high content of quartz (more than 10 per cent) and feldspar. When it crystallizes, the glassy quartz and beige-coloured feldspar make the rock very pale. Acid intrusive rock includes granite (shown here). Its extrusive equivalent is rhyolite.

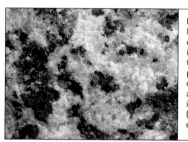

INTERMEDIATE
Magma containing 55–65 per cent silica forms rock called intermediate rock. It is darker than acid rock because it has less pale-coloured quartz and more darker-coloured minerals, such as hornblende. Intermediate intrusive rock includes diorite (shown here). The surface equivalent of diorite is andesite.

BASIC
Magma with 45–55 per cent silica, forms basic rock, which is dark or even black. At the surface, basic lava typically forms fine-grained basalt, the most common igneous rock. In sills and dykes just below the surface, basic magma forms medium-grained dolerite, while deeper down it forms coarse-grained gabbro (shown here).

ULTRABASIC
Igneous rocks that contain less than 45 per cent silica and no feldspar minerals are known as ultrabasic. Rocks such as peridotite (shown here) and pyroxenite are composed mostly of pyroxene and olivine. Peridotite is a relatively rare rock, which is brought up from the mantle during continental collisions.

HALF DOME, YOSEMITE ▲
Yosemite's Half Dome, in California's Sierra Nevada range, is a dramatic example of an exposed batholith (*see* p.25). A large mass of magma solidified underground about 50 million years ago and was gradually exposed over millions of years as the softer (non-igneous) overlying rock weathered away. The much harder granodiorite (a mixture of granite and diorite) Dome was eventually left behind and then carved in half by a glacier.

AMYGDALES IN BASALT

Some igneous rock, such as basalt and andesite, can contain pockets of other minerals known as amygdales. Amygdales form from gas bubbles in the magma. The word "amygdale" comes from the Latin for "almond". Typically, the mineral-rich liquid trapped in the bubbles forms minerals called zeolites.

Zeolite

Granite rock ensures sculptures will last a long time

METAMORPHIC ROCK

Metamorphic rock is rock that has been changed beyond recognition by exposure to intense heat or pressure or both. Contact metamorphism happens when rock comes into contact with the searing heat of the red-hot magma found in an igneous intrusion. The extreme temperatures can realign the crystals within the rock so much that it can change into a new rock, such as marble or hornfels, depending on the intensity of the heat.

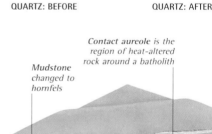

QUARTZ: BEFORE   QUARTZ: AFTER

◀ SHOCK METAMORPHISM
Not all contact metamorphism is caused by volcanic activity. When a meteorite hurtles into the Earth, the impact sends tremendous shockwaves through the ground, squeezing the rock to two or three times its original density. This micrograph shows the changes to the quartz's crystal structure.

Contact aureole is the region of heat-altered rock around a batholith

Mudstone changed to hornfels

HORNFELS: CHANGED FROM MUDSTONE

Sandstone changed to metaquartzite

Limestone changed to marble

More distant mudstone changed to "spotted" rock

Hot magma of granite or gabbro batholith

▲ CONTACT METAMORPHISM
The scorching heat of a large magma batholith transforms the rocks around it. The closer the rocks are to the batholith, and the larger the batholith, the more they are altered by the heat. Sandstone changes to hard quartzite. Limestone turns to brilliant white or banded marble. Closer to the edges of the batholith, mudstone turns to dark, splintery hornfels. Further away some minerals are left unaltered, and some new ones grow, creating "spotted" rock.

HUGE FORCES ▶
The temperatures and pressures involved in metamorphism are enormous. As a result, the rocks produced by these forces are very tough and can withstand erosion over millions of years. Some metamorphism takes place deep underground. Here the Earth's tectonic plates move with enough force to open abysses in the ocean floor or throw up giant mountain ranges, such as Greenland's Stauning Alps (shown here).

Garnet crystals

metamorphic
rock

Schist *created from mudstone*

▲ NEW CRYSTALS

Molten magma is so hot that it can virtually melt the surrounding country rock – rock that existed before metamorphism occurred – allowing entirely new crystals to form. Minerals such as andalusite, kyanite, and sillimanite are clear signs of metamorphic rock, because they only form at high temperatures and pressures. Some beautiful gem crystals are formed this way, such as the almandine garnets embedded in this schist rock – a form of highly metamorphosed mudstone.

◀ SANDSTONE TO QUARTZITE

The quartz grains in sandstone are so tough that the heat of metamorphism has little effect – simply forging sandstone (shown left) into a much tougher rock called quartzite (show right). Quartzite can look a little like hard brown sugar. It is so hard that quartzites in Western Australia are among the oldest rocks on Earth, dating from around 3.5 billion years ago.

◀ LIMESTONE TO MARBLE

Limestone (shown left) and dolomite are transformed into marble (shown right) by exposure to intense heat and pressure. Limestone is rich in calcite (calcium carbonate), which comes from living matter. Limestones are dull and powdery, but contact metamorphism transforms them into tough, white marble.

Carrara's bright white marble *is highly prized for its purity*

Checking the marble *to ensure it has no faults or colouring minerals*

MARBLE QUARRY IN CARRARA ▲

In mountain-building regions, contact and regional metamorphism (where enormous pressure is felt over a large area) can recrystallize the calcite in limestone, transforming it into marble. The purer the limestone is, the whiter the marble. The brilliant white marble from Carrara in Italy's Apennine mountain region is considered the most perfect marble of all and was cherished by Renaissance sculptors, such as Michelangelo. Impurities in the original limestone (such as silica and iron) give marble its distinctive coloured streaks.

Michelangelo's *David is carved from a single, carefully selected block of Carrara marble*

REGIONAL METAMORPHISM

The tremendous forces involved when continents collide can crush and bake rocks over a large region, metamorphosing rocks over a wide area. Sometimes, regional metamorphism can create similar rocks to those produced by contact metamorphism. But at other times the metamorphism is much more intense creating entirely new kinds of rock. The most extreme metamorphism creates its own unique banding structures.

GRADES OF METAMORPHISM

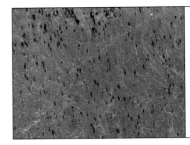

SLATE (LOW)
Mudstone is transformed into flaky, grey slate by low-grade regional metamorphism. High pressure and low temperatures realign minerals found in clay, such as mica and chlorite, into flat layers.

PHYLLITE (LOW)
Like slate, phyllite is created by mild regional metamorphism of mudstone or shale. But the effect is more intense – the mica flakes are larger and more visible and develop a silky, mirror-like sheen.

SCHIST (MEDIUM)
Medium-grade metamorphism creates the rock schist by realigning crystals of chlorite and mica into bands sandwiched between bands of quartz and feldspar. The banding is called schistosity.

GNEISS (HIGH)
Gneiss is formed by the highest grade of metamorphism. Extreme heat and pressure create a glittering rock in which entirely new crystals form in alternating wave-like dark and light bands.

COLLISION ZONE METAMORPHISM ▶
When two of the Earth's tectonic plates crunch together, it creates the perfect conditions for metamorphism. As a moving ocean plate is forced downwards, the edge of the continental plate is subjected to tremendous heat and pressure. Conditions like this produce deeply altered and contorted rocks such as schists and gneisses. Often, the rocks are altered not just once but many times, as they are subjected to continuing pressures.

High pressure and low temperature create schist

Continental crust showing folding at point of impact

CONTINENTAL PLATE

OCEANIC PLATE

Molten layer

Subducted plate

High pressure and high temperature close to the molten layer create gneiss

Ancient metamorphic rocks raised up into mountain peaks

Frost opens up cracks in the toughest rocks

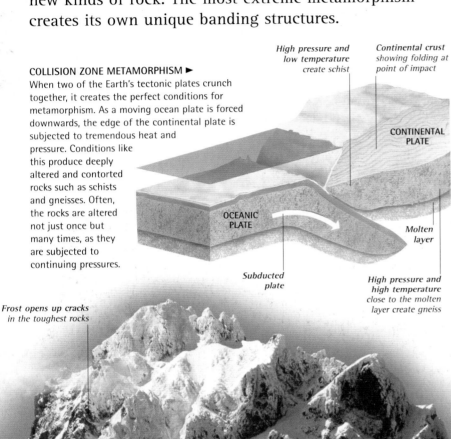

▲ THE ANDES
The mighty Andes in South America are made from ancient sediments, metamorphosed into tough quartzite and slate tens of millions of years ago. These rocks were then thrown up by colliding plates to create the world's longest mountain range. The huge forces involved are also creating new metamorphic rock deep underground in the mountain's roots. One day, these too will be exposed on the surface.

Close-up of gneiss showing dark biotite mica

FOLIATION ►
Rocks metamorphosed from mudstone and shale are often marked by flat or wavy lines called foliation. The dark lines are created when bands of sheet-like minerals, such as mica, are squeezed flat by the pressure. Slate, phyllite, schist, and gneiss all have foliations like this. Rocks metamorphosed from limestone (marble), sandstone (quartzite), and coal (anthracite) have none of these foliations, and the interlocking crystal grains show no specific pattern. This is called a granular texture.

Gneiss in cliff-face shows bands of quartz and feldspar

at cleavage planes, where slate is easily broken

◄ SLATE QUARRY IN WALES
In slate, all the minerals are dark grey and fine-grained. Foliation of slate does not create alternate dark and light bands. Instead, pressure realigns the mica and chlorite minerals into layers. This creates a rock that cleaves (splits) easily into smooth, flat sheets, some of which can be huge. This slate quarry is in Wales, a country that was once world-famous for its slate industry.

SPLITTING SLATE

Slate is brittle and flakes easily, but it is also very weather resistant. The combination of weather resistance and the ease with which it can be broken into flat sheets made slate the perfect roofing material. During the 19th and 20th centuries, it was used for roofing vast numbers of new houses in Europe and the USA. Slatemakers were highly skilled craftsmen who were able to split blocks of stone into smooth, thin rectangular tiles using just a hammer and chisel.

Dramatic folding of layers of mudstone and sandstone

FOLDED GNEISS

Separate bands of pale and dark minerals

e ▶▶
metamorphic rock

FOLDING ►
In folded gneiss, the separated bands of dark hornblende and mica and pale quartz and feldspar minerals can be clearly seen. Folding is when rock layers are contorted by plate movements, which are not powerful enough to alter the actual composition of the rock, shown here in these folded cliffs from South Wales, UK.

SEDIMENTARY ROCK

Sedimentary rock, formed from the debris of other rocks and living matter, is the third basic rock type. Although it only makes up five per cent of the Earth's crust by volume it covers about 75 per cent of the Earth's land surface. Sedimentary rock can be divided into three categories: detrital (from rock particles), chemical or inorganic (from particles that can dissolve in water), and organic (from plant remains). Some sedimentary rock contains fossils, which provide vital clues to understanding Earth's geological history.

◄ LAYERS OF SEDIMENT

When rock is exposed to the elements – wind, rain, and repeated cycles of freezing and thawing – it slowly erodes. The debris is carried away by water, wind, and ice and deposited in layers. Over time these layers are buried by more sediments and eventually harden into sedimentary rock. When sedimentary rock is exposed in cross-section as here, you can see the layers in which the sediments have been deposited, one on top of the other.

sedimentary rock

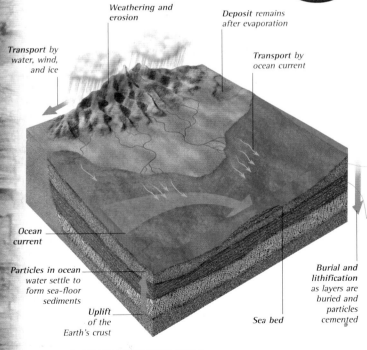

Weathering and erosion

Deposit remains after evaporation

Transport by water, wind, and ice

Transport by ocean current

Ocean current

Particles in ocean water settle to form sea-floor sediments

Uplift of the Earth's crust

Sea bed

Burial and lithification as layers are buried and particles cemented

▲ SEDIMENTARY (DETRITAL) ROCK CYCLE

In this phase of the rock cycle, detrital sedimentary rock forms from millions of rock particles. These particles are transported by wind, water, and ice, before being deposited as sediments on the beds of oceans, lakes, and rivers. Layer is buried by layer, until the particles are cemented together by a combination of the weight of the layers above and minerals deposited from water moving through the sediments. Over millions of years, the layers form sedimentary rock.

PARTICLE SIZE FOR DETRITAL ROCKS

BOULDERS
Detrital rocks are composed of many particle sizes, ranging from microscopic (clay) to huge (boulders). Boulders – rocks more than 25 cm (10 in) across – tend to be moved only by glaciers. When smaller boulders combine with finer particles they form a "mixture" called conglomerate.

COBBLES
Cobbles range in size from 6 cm to 25 cm (2¹/₂–10 in) across. Strong forces sort particles by size, so they are often found in high-energy environments such as fast-flowing rivers and landslides. Cobbles can combine to form conglomerate or breccia – see opposite.

PEBBLES
Pebbles, the typical particles found in conglomerates, range in size from 4 mm to 60 mm (¹/₆–2¹/₂ in). Any sharp edges are gradually smoothed as the pebbles are continuously rolled and bounced along rivers and seashores, suggesting a long period of transport.

SAND
Below pebble come gravel and then sand particles. Sand particles can be up to 2 mm (¹/₁₂ in) and can still be seen by the naked eye. Sand particles are found in a number of environments, ranging from mountain lakes to the ocean floor. They combine to form sandstone.

SILT
Silt particles are smaller than sand and can no longer be seen with the naked eye. The result of prolonged weathering, silt particles usually settle in quiet riverbeds with little or no current. They combine with clay to form fine-grained rocks such as mudstone and shale.

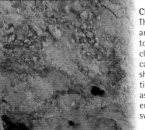

CLAY
The smallest particles of all are clay. Little energy is needed to transport clay particles, so clay settles very slowly and is carried out furthest from the shore. Accumulation of these tiny particles is usually associated with quiet environments such as lakes, swamps, or lagoons.

▲ BEDDING WITH UNCONFORMITY

Sedimentary rocks form when layers of sediment are laid down in beds. This layering is one of the most characteristic features of sedimentary rock. Each layer is unique, with variations in composition and thickness reflecting the different conditions under which it was deposited. A bedding plane – the boundary between two layers of sedimentary rock – is usually visible as a line across the rock. Unconformities are breaks in the regular pattern of beds, which show where a new phase of rock-building has begun on top of older rock.

▲ CROSS BEDDING

Most layers are deposited horizontally since sediments usually accumulate as particles from a fluid. Sometimes sediments do not settle in horizontal layers. If sloping beds form across and within the main bed, the result is known as cross bedding. This is a characteristic feature of sand-dune, river-delta, and stream-channel environments. The distinctive pattern in this eroded Navajo sandstone from Colorado, USA, is caused by the currents moving in different directions at different times.

◄ MUDSTONE

The fine-grained group of rocks that includes mudstone, shale, and siltstone are the most common sedimentary rocks. Mudstone breaks into chunks or blocks, while shale splits in layers.

◄ CONGLOMERATE

Conglomerates are formed when rounded particles of pebble size and larger become cemented together in a fine-silt matrix. They are very hard. Pebbly-sized conglomerates were once used for grinding grain.

Fine matrix of sediments binds rock fragments together

Angular fragments of granite and other rock

LOESS ►

Loess is dust and silt that probably originated on the margins of retreating ice sheets. It can be blown by the wind over great distances forming extremely fertile soils. Estimates suggest that 10 per cent of Earth's surface is covered by large loess deposits, such as those found in northern China.

◄ SANDSTONE

Quartz is the predominant mineral in most sandstone. Sandstones that contain feldspar are called arkose, while those formed from a mixture of particles are called greywacke. Sandstone carves easily and resists weathering.

BRECCIA ►

When the large particles in the rock mixture are angular rather than rounded, the rock is called breccia. Most breccias form in mountain regions, where the freeze-thaw cycle breaks the rocks into coarse, sharp-edged pieces. These can gather in cone-shaped deposits at the foot of steep slopes.

CHEMICAL SEDIMENTS

Detrital sedimentary rocks are formed from fragments of rock, and you can often see the original mineral grains or even entire pebbles in them. But sedimentary rocks made through the action of chemicals in the earth have a powdery texture with no trace of the original fragments. These rocks are formed from minerals like calcite that dissolve in water. These dissolved minerals may create solid deposits, or precipitates. Some precipitates simply fill in the spaces in other sediments; some form entirely new rocks, such as limestone.

OOLITIC LIMESTONE ▶
Oolitic limestone is made from tiny balls of calcite called ooliths. Ooliths are made when calcite precipitates out of lime-saturated water and sticks to tiny grains of silt that roll about in underwater currents. The word oolith comes from the Greek word for "egg". This rock is also known as roe limestone after its resemblance to fish roe (eggs).

OOLITH FORMATION ▲
Ooliths form in shallow, carbonate-rich tropical waters like these in the Bahamas. Wherever oolitic limestone appears, it is evidence that conditions were like this millions of years ago. The famous oolitic limestones of Kansas, USA, and Dorset, England, formed in conditions like these.

Oolitic "balls" formed by calcite deposits

Saw-edged ridges caused by chemical weathering

Compact carbonate rock

▲ DOLOMITIC LIMESTONE
In shallow tropical seas with plenty of evaporation, carbonate minerals may be precipitated on the seabed. These deposits eventually turn into limestone. When the predominant carbonate is calcium, it forms limestone. When it is magnesium (common in sea water), it forms dolomitic limestone.

THE DOLOMITES ▶
The term dolomitic comes from the Dolomite range in northern Italy, at the eastern end of the Alps. Like all Alpine sediments, the limestone in the Dolomites formed on the bed of the sea that once lay between northern Europe and Africa. But over millions of years, the pressure of the north-moving African plate threw it upward to create the dramatic mountains seen today.

Tufa formations

▲ TUFA TOWERS IN MONO LAKE, CALIFORNIA

Tufas are white, knobbly rocks formed from deposits of calcite (calcium carbonate). They typically form around springs, or in caves, on stalagmites and stalactites. Where springs rich in calcium bubble into lakes rich in carbonate, towers of tufa may form as the calcium combines with the carbonate. The towers grow underwater, but in California's Mono Lake they have become visible as water levels have dropped. The Trona Pinnacles area of California's Mojave Desert has tufa towers up to 43 m (140 ft) high, left behind by the evaporation of ancient lakes.

MINERAL FORMATIONS IN SEDIMENTARY ROCK

SEPTARIAN NODULE
Nodules are tough balls of mineral that form in sedimentary rock. Septarian nodules began as mudballs that formed around decomposing sea life. When they dried out, they filled with minerals, such as dolomite. These minerals in turn cracked, and the cracks filled with veins of calcite (shown here in white).

FLINT
Flint nodules appear in chalk and other limestones. They form when bubbles of silica-rich fluid – from the remains of sea sponges – solidified. On the outside they are nobbly, white pebbles, but inside they look like brown glass. They fracture with such a sharp edge that they were used as knives in the Stone Age.

PYRITE NODULE
Pyrite nodules are frequently mistaken for meteorites because of their shape. They are often found in mudstone and shale, where long, radiating, needle-like crystals of iron pyrite form around a mineral fragment. Pyrite makes sparks when struck on stone, and pyrite nodules were probably humankind's earliest firelighters.

Crude salt starting to crystallize at lake edge

▲ EVAPORITES IN QINGHAI SALT LAKE, CHINA

Evaporites are salts that were once dissolved in water. When the water in which they were dissolved evaporates, they are left behind as deposits. Typically, the minerals in evaporites are halite (rock salt) and gypsum. They are common where sea water evaporates in lagoons, and around the salty lakes of desert regions, such as the Great Salt Lake, Utah, USA, and the Qinghai Salt Lake in China.

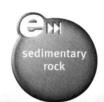

sedimentary rock

Dramatic, jagged landscape caused by chemical erosion of limestone

KARST LANDSCAPE ▶

The Stone Forest of Yunnan Province, China, is a striking example of karst scenery. Karst gets its name from the distinctive limestone formations found in the Karst region of Slovenia. The limestone is easily dissolved by acid rainwater seeping down through cracks in the rock. These fantastic shapes are the result of tens of thousands of years of chemical corrosion.

CAVES

Many mountains, hills, and cliffs contain natural holes or caves. The largest and most common caves are those that form when rock is dissolved by chemicals in water trickling through it. These are called solution caves. They are typical of limestone regions, where the rock is often hollowed out into spectacular caverns. But caves can also form in other ways. Sea caves, for instance, are hollowed out of sea cliffs where pounding waves have opened up cracks. Ice caves are formed by ice melting under glaciers. Lava caves are tunnels left behind by hot lava in lava flows.

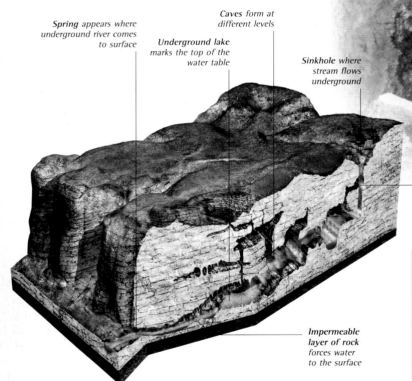

Spring appears where underground river comes to surface

Caves form at different levels

Underground lake marks the top of the water table

Sinkhole where stream flows underground

Pothole where water plunges down a vertical shaft

Gallery full of unusual calcite mineral formations such as this arch

Stalactites hang from the cavern roof

Impermeable layer of rock forces water to the surface

▲ CAVE SYSTEM

There is little surface water in limestone country because the water seeps away so easily through joints (cracks) in limestone. Streams mostly plunge down through potholes, and as the water flows downwards, so acid in it dissolves the rocks and widens pipe-like channels into tunnels and caves. At a certain point, the water meets the water table – the level up to which the rock is permanently soaked with groundwater. This is where the largest caves occur. The water table fluctuates with changing weather, so new caves form at different levels. Over thousands of years, complex, multi-level cave systems can develop, such as the famous Mammoth Caves in Kentucky, USA.

caves

CAVE PAINTING FROM LASCAUX

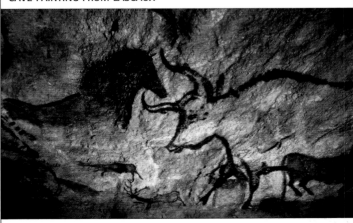

In prehistoric times, people often took shelter in caves. Evidence of this comes from the artefacts and cave art they left behind, especially in western Europe, China, and southern Africa. Although these people are sometimes referred to as cavemen, they did not live in caves. Instead, they used them for shelter from bad weather and for defense from predatory animals. Deep inside these caves, early people painted pictures of animals and hunting scenes, which may have had a religious significance. Some of the best-known cave paintings are found in Lascaux, France, which were painted some 17,000 years ago.

SPELEOTHEMS

STALAGMITES

Stalagmites are dramatic rock spikes and columns, built up from calcite-rich water dripping onto the cavern floor. As the water evaporates (dries up) in the air of the cavern, it deposits calcite, which slowly accumulates, growing into a higher and higher structure. When a stalagmite grows tall enough to meet a descending stalactite, it forms a pillar as shown here. This 27-m (89-ft)-tall Monarch pillar is from the Carlsbad Caverns, a huge complex of limestone caverns and tunnels, which extends for more than 50 km (30 miles) in New Mexico, USA.

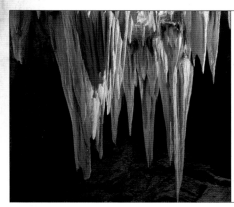

STALACTITES

Stalactites are spectacular icicle-like features that form as water slowly drips down from the cavern roof. A stalactite grows, literally, drip by drip. Before it drops to the cavern floor, each drip clings for a while to the tip of the stalactite and leaves a calcite deposit at the rim. The next drip forms in the same place and also leaves a deposit. Very slowly, these rim deposits build up to form a tube. This is why many stalactites are hollow or partially hollow at their centre. The world's longest stalactite, at Poll-an-Ionain in County Clare, Ireland, is 6.2 m (20 ft) long.

CAVE PEARLS

Cave pearls are quite rare, appearing as rounded, white pebbles in small pools of water. They form when water dripping into the pool loses carbon dioxide and deposits calcite in layers around a grain of sand or tiny rock fragment. Movement of the water rolls the growing pearl around, and eventually it forms a perfect, polished sphere. All the time the pearl gathers more and more layers of calcite, until after thousands of years it becomes too heavy for the water to move it and becomes fixed. Sometimes spectacular "nests" of these pearls form in cave pools, as shown here.

Stalagmites grow up from the floor

▲ UNDERGROUND PALACE

Limestone caverns can become spectacular natural palaces, such as the Yunshui caverns in Fangshan county, near Beijing, China, shown here lit with coloured lights. These caverns are covered in different kinds of calcite (calcium carbonate) deposits, collectively called speleothems. They are created by the constant dripping of water that is saturated in calcite, which has dissolved from the limestone. The larger cave deposits create an interior of pillars and platforms. The colours vary from alabaster white to a dusky red caused by iron deposits. The best-known cave structures are stalactites and stalagmites. Twisting structures are called helictites.

SINKHOLES ▶

When acidic rainwater creates limestone caves close to the ground surface, the cave roof may become so thin that it suddenly collapses, forming a sinkhole. While everything may look solid on the surface, changing conditions, such as urban development or a heavy rainstorm, can trigger the collapse. This large sinkhole has opened up in the arid, treeless Nullarbor Plain in Western Australia.

Sinkhole caused by cavern collapsing near surface

▲ DESERT OASIS

Groundwater is all the water that is stored underground in the soil or in permeable rock – rock that allows water to trickle through it. Typically, groundwater appears on the surface where a hollow in the ground allows the water table to rise, as it does in this oasis in the Namibian Desert in southern Africa. Groundwater can appear when heavy rain or melting snow raises the water table, creating a spring, a well, or even a lake.

HOW FOSSILS FORM

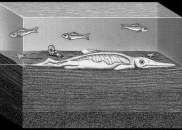

Ichthyosaurus decays and is buried in soft sediments on the sea floor

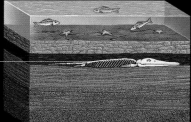

Layers of sediment cover the reptile's bones, which are gradually mineralized

Weight of land compresses the fossilized skeleton

Forces of erosion wear away the surface, exposing the skeleton

FOSSILS

Nearly all sedimentary rock contains fossils, the preserved remains of plants and animals that lived millions of years ago when the rocks were formed. Fossils are perhaps the geologist's most useful clues to the history behind rock formation. Most of the fossils are shellfish, such as ammonites, which lived in shallow seas. Many of these fossils are characteristic of a particular geological period, so that they can help to date precisely the rock in which they are found.

Preserved footprint of carnivorous theropod dinosaur, possibly an Allosaurus

◄ FOSSILIZATION OF AN ICHTHYOSAURUS

Fossils form in a number of ways, but normally only the hard parts of an animal, such as its bones or shell are preserved. Soft parts usually rot before they can be fossilized. This sequence shows how an ancient marine reptile called an *Ichthyosaurus* may have fossilized in mud on the sea floor.

▲ TRACE FOSSILS

Trace fossils are not the fossils of an animal's remains, but preserve the signs left behind by the animal, such as a nest or footprints. Perfectly preserved footprints (shown above) reveal the tracks of a three-toed theropod dinosaur as it tramped across mudflats more than 170 million years ago.

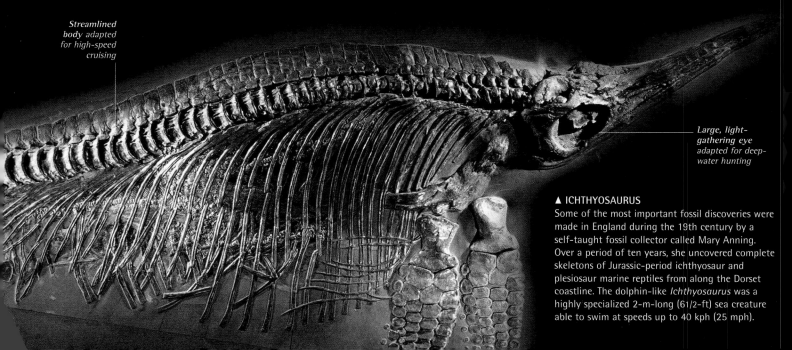

Streamlined body adapted for high-speed cruising

Large, light-gathering eye adapted for deep-water hunting

▲ ICHTHYOSAURUS

Some of the most important fossil discoveries were made in England during the 19th century by a self-taught fossil collector called Mary Anning. Over a period of ten years, she uncovered complete skeletons of Jurassic-period ichthyosaur and plesiosaur marine reptiles from along the Dorset coastline. The dolphin-like *Ichthyosaurus* was a highly specialized 2-m-long (61/2-ft) sea creature able to swim at speeds up to 40 kph (25 mph).

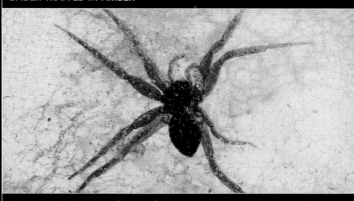

SPIDER TRAPPED IN AMBER

Amber is the fossilized resin (sticky sap) produced by some species of pine tree. Since prehistoric times, its attractive yellow appearance has led to its use in jewellery and religious objects. Insects are so fragile that they are rarely preserved as fossils. However, they can become preserved in amber (along with lichens, small lizards, and frogs) for millions of years. They become trapped in the sticky resin as it drips down trunks and stems before hardening. Sometimes even the delicate veins of insect wings survive. Amber is extremely useful for ancient DNA research as it preserves soft tissue for a very long time. In most fossilized bones, all the organic material is replaced by minerals.

▲ ANCIENT SHELLFISH

Ammonites are extinct shellfish related to cuttlefish and squid. These creatures were on Earth for around 160 million years until the end of the Cretaceous period, 65 million years ago. They were so widespread and varied, evolving rapidly all the time, that they have become a key guide for geologists, indicating exactly when a rock formed.

▲ FOSSIL FERNS

One of the key pieces of evidence that dinosaurs were killed off by a global climatic disaster was the discovery of "fern spikes". Dating from a short period just after the extinction, these are fossils which show large concentrations of ferns. Ferns are often the first plants to return after volcanic eruptions or other geological catastrophes.

A 70-cm-long (2-ft) nose gave T. rex *an acute sense of smell*

Plaster jacket used to protect exposed T. rex *thigh bone*

Serrated, curved 18-cm-long (7-inch) teeth

Lower jaw hinged in the middle like a door

▲ THE FOSSIL RECORD

Discovering a major fossil like this 80-million-year-old *T. rex* thigh bone is an exciting event. As well as telling us a little more about dinosaurs, it also helps us to build up a fossil record of how life evolved over time. Fossils can also reveal the movements of Earth's landmasses and changes in the Earth's climate, from almost desertlike to the bitter cold of the Ice Ages. Fossils can even reveal the existence of catastrophic events that caused mass extinctions of life, such as the one that killed off the dinosaurs 65 million years ago.

T. REX SKULL ▶

Dinosaur fossils are rare, but when found – in places such as the Badlands of the American Midwest and Asia's Gobi Desert – they are often spectacular. Fossils of more than 350 different kinds of dinosaur have been found to date, ranging from tiny two-legged runners to gigantic, lumbering four-legged vegetarians. Fossils are rarely complete skeletons, so the discovery of the complete skull of a *Tyrannosaurus rex*, like this one found in the Black Hills of South Dakota, USA, is a major event. *T. rex* was the second-largest flesh-eater that ever lived – taller than a house and heavier than an elephant.

fossils

Chalk layers built up from the crushed shells of microscopic sea creatures

ROCK FROM LIFE-FORMS

Some of the world's toughest rock, including many kinds of limestone, is made from the remains of living things. There are two kinds of organic sedimentary rock: bioclastic and biogenic. Bioclastic rock, such as limestone, is made from the fragmented remains of plants and sea creatures. Biogenic rock, such as coral, is made from the whole remains of living things. Sometimes the buried remains of living organisms are transformed over millions of years into fossil fuels, such as coal, oil, and natural gas.

◀ WHITE CLIFFS OF DOVER
Chalk, here exposed in England's White Cliffs of Dover, is a soft white rock of almost pure calcite (calcium carbonate). It formed on the seabed some 100 million years ago during the Cretaceous period, when dinosaurs roamed the Earth. Minute algae grew with coccoliths (microscopic plates of calcite). When the algae died, the plates fell on the sea floor along with the shells from tiny animals called foraminifers. These eventually turned into chalk.

sedimentary rock

Foraminiferal shells are microfossils found in chalk formed on the seabed.

▲ FOSSILIFEROUS LIMESTONE
Most limestones are a mixture of organic and chemically formed calcite. But a few, like fossiliferous limestone, are made almost entirely of fossils, like this 420-million-year-old example of Silurian limestone from Wenlock in Shropshire, England. It is rich in sea-creature fossils, such as trilobites (beetle-like creatures, now extinct) and brachiopods – a type of shellfish that was attached to the sea floor by a stalk.

▲ FOSSILIZED ORGANISMS IN CHALK
The fossilized remains of coccoliths (algae plates) and sea creatures (foraminifers – shown here) that make up chalk are so tiny that the rock looks white and powdery. But under a powerful microscope, the organisms can be seen. Unlike most protozoans (single-celled organisms), foraminifers have shells and it is their shells – along with the plates of calcite deposited by algae – that are preserved as calcite in chalk.

CORAL REEFS

Reef, or coral, limestones are made entirely from the fossilized remains of the creatures that lived on coral reefs, including the corals themselves, millions of years ago. Sometimes the shape of the ancient reef may be preserved in the formation of the rock, which forms a small hill called a reef knoll. The best-known coral reef is the Great Barrier Reef off the eastern coast of Australia.

Corals are formed from the external skeletons of marine animals.

THE STORY OF COAL

① Warm swamps in Carboniferous period turn to peat

Vegetation dies and falls into the swamp.

PEAT

② Lignite formed from peat buried deep in mud

LIGNITE

③ Bituminous coal produced after hundreds of millions of years of pressure

BITUMINOUS COAL

④ Anthracite produced by extreme pressure on coal

ANTHRACITE

◄ COAL FROM DEAD PLANTS

Coal is made from plants that grew in swamps millions of years ago. As time passed, dead layers of these plants were squeezed dry by the weight of mud above them and they turned to increasingly concentrated carbon. At the top is soft brown peat (60 per cent carbon). Lower down is more compressed, dull brown coal or lignite (73 per cent carbon), then shiny black, bituminous coal (83 per cent carbon). Anthracite (almost 100 per cent carbon) only forms under extreme pressure.

▲ MINING COAL

The best coal (bituminous and anthracite) is usually found in narrow layers called seams, far below ground. To get at this coal, engineers sink deep shafts to reach the seam. Miners then tunnel along it to extract the coal from the exposed face. This coal face at Blacksville, Virginia, USA, is 240 m (800 ft) below ground. In the past, coal was dug out by hand with picks and shovels. Most modern pits now use remote-controlled cutting machines, such as the longwall shearer shown here.

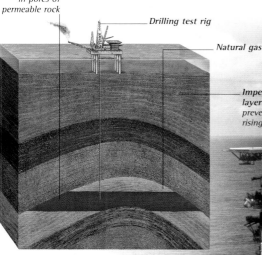

Oil trapped in pores of permeable rock

Drilling test rig

Natural gas

Derrick holds the boring pipe. It is lengthened as the drill goes deeper

Impervious layer of rock prevents oil rising

Excess gas burner

▲ OIL TRAPS

Most oil comes from tiny organisms that lived in the sea millions of years ago. When their remains were buried in seabed mud, bacteria turned them to kerogen (a waxy, tarlike substance). Over time, heat and pressure deep below the surface turned the kerogen into oil and natural gas. Most of this oil becomes trapped in a layer of porous rock (rock that holds liquid) under layers of impervious rock (rock that does not allow liquid to pass through it).

◄ DRILLING FOR OIL

When oil is found under the seabed, a drilling tower, known as a derrick, is set up on an oil rig. Some oil rigs are floating platforms; others are anchored to the seabed, such as this one in the North Sea. The choice of rig depends on the seabed, the depth of water, and the usual weather conditions. Often a single oil rig can open up a number of wells, by sending the drill bits down at an angle into the oil trap.

SPACE ROCK

Earth's geology is far from unique. Earth is one of four rock planets circling the Sun, along with Mercury, Venus, and Mars. The Moon is also rocky. The Earth is continually being struck by space rocks known as meteorites. Some kinds of meteorites, called chondrites, appear to have changed little since they were formed in the earliest days of the Solar System. Geochemists believe that when they look at a particular kind of chondrite meteorite, called a carbonaceous chondrite, they are looking at the earliest form of rock.

▲ SHOOTING STARS IN EARTH'S ATMOSPHERE

Most meteorites come from fragments of asteroids – large bodies of space rock. In space these fragments are known as meteoroids. When they enter the Earth's atmosphere they become meteors. Most meteors are so tiny they burn up on entry, creating the glowing trails we call shooting stars. When the Earth passes through the tail of a comet (an icy lump which releases vast clouds of gas and dust as it approaches the Sun), meteor showers (shooting stars) like those shown here can be seen in the night sky. Occasionally, meteors are so large that they crash into the Earth without burning up entirely – these are called meteorites.

Martian rock from meteorite

▲ MARTIAN METEORITES ON EARTH

Twenty-four of the meteorites found on Earth originally came from Mars. They are the only samples of rock that we have from another planet. This one, found in the icy Antarctic desert, caused tremendous excitement when NASA scientists found microscopic structures in it. They believed these could only have been created by living organisms. Future space probes to Mars will look for signs of microscopic life on the planet.

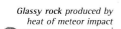
Glassy rock produced by heat of meteor impact

Tektites are often egg-shaped

▲ TEKTITES

Tektites are small blobs of silica-rich glassy rock, which are usually disc- or egg-shaped. They can vary in colour from pale yellow to black. Geologists once thought them to be meteorite fragments, but now reckon they are produced when molten blobs of terrestrial rock, flung out by the impact of a huge meteorite, rapidly cool.

METEOR CRATER ▶

There are many more meteorite craters on the Moon than on the Earth. Geologists suggest that the reason we do not see as many impact craters here is because continual geological activity covers them up. Nevertheless, some can be seen. The first impact crater to be identified was Meteor Crater in the Arizona desert, USA (shown here). It was created 49,000 years ago by a 305,000-tonne (300,000-ton)-meteorite which hit the Earth at around 724,000 kph (450,000 mph). Scientists have identified more than 160 large impact sites around the world.

TYPES OF METEORITE

IRONS
Meteorites are made from iron and stone. They are divided into three groups according to how much of each they contain. Irons – or iron-nickels – are less common than stones, but were the first to be identified because their metallic look and weight made them easy to recognize. The largest meteorites are irons.

STONES
Almost 90 per cent of the meteorites that fall to Earth are stones. They range from ancient chondrites, as old as the Solar System itself, to rocks that have broken off the Moon and Mars. Chondrites, like the one shown here, get their name because they contain chondrules – once-molten globules of pyroxene or olivine.

STONY IRONS
These are the least common of all meteorites and less than 10 tonnes (9.8 tons) of them have been found. The stony-iron group is very varied, but the one thing these rocks have in common is that they are all about half iron-nickel and half stone. Stony irons are divided into pallasites (shown here) and mesosiderites.

VOLANOES IN SPACE

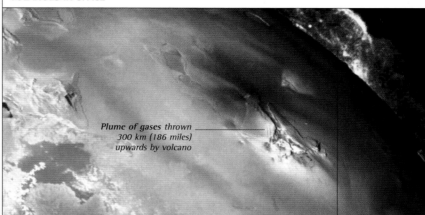

Plume of gases thrown 300 km (186 miles) upwards by volcano

Io's surface pulsates as it is squeezed by Jupiter's gravity

Earth is not the only planet in the Solar System with volcanoes. Mars has Olympus Mons, the tallest volcano in the Solar System, and Venus has more volcanoes than any other planet. But the most spectacular volcanic activity is found on Jupiter's moon Io. It is probably not Io's internal heat that generates volcanic activity, but the closeness of Jupiter. The giant planet's intense gravitational pull creates so much pressure on Io that it melts rock. Some parts of Io brighten regularly as floods of lava erupt from the surface. One volcano, called Loki, has a cauldron of lava 200 km (120 miles) across.

space rock

Reddish tinge comes from high iron content of Martian rock

MARTIAN ROCKS ▲
We know more about the planet Mars than any other planet. The search for signs of life there has prompted a series of exploratory missions to the planet. We know that Mars has a rocky composition very similar to Earth's, with an iron core, a semi-molten mantle, and a hard crust. Unmanned missions are revealing more and more evidence that water once flowed on the surface of Mars – and if there was water, there could have been life. Photographs from above the surface have revealed vast valleys that look as if they were carved out by floodwater. In 2004, NASA's robotic Mars rovers *Spirit* and *Opportunity* analysed Martian rocks, which showed signs that they were once covered in water.

Breccia (rock fragments) fall back into the crater after impact

Rim built up from ejecta – pulverized rock blasted out by the impact

1.2 KM (3/4 MILE)

MINERAL CLASSES

To make sense of the 3,000 or so different kinds of mineral, mineralogists organize them into classes, or families, based on their chemical composition. The most widely used system for grouping minerals is the Dana system. First published by Yale University professor James Dana in 1848, this system divides minerals into eight basic classes. The most important groupings are native elements, silicates, oxides, sulphides, sulphates, halides, carbonates, and phosphates. Dana's system is still used today.

Carnelian is a rare mineral that forms in veins of hot fluid

CARNELIAN VEIN IN ROCK CRYSTAL

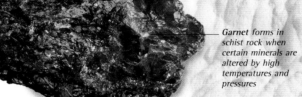

Garnet forms in schist rock when certain minerals are altered by high temperatures and pressures

GARNET IN SCHIST

▲ HOW MINERALS FORM
Minerals form when the elements in a gas or liquid crystallize into a solid. Different combinations of elements form different minerals. Some form when hot, molten rock from the Earth's interior cools slowly; others form from chemicals dissolved in liquids in the ground. Existing minerals can be altered by chemicals in the Earth or be transformed by being squeezed or heated by geological processes such as mountain building. The rocks of the Earth's crust are made of common minerals; rarer minerals tend to form in veins (cracks) and cavities (holes) in the rocks.

EVAPORITES ▲
When hot, mineral-rich, salty waters evaporate (dry up), the minerals left behind are known as evaporites. Halite, gypsum, and anhydrite form in this way. Most evaporites form around hot springs – spouts of water heated by volcanic activity. At Pamukkale, Turkey (pictured above), mineral deposits from calcite-rich hot springs have created a solid white "waterfall" made from the evaporite, travertine.

MINERAL CLASSES

NATIVE (*see* pp.50–53)
Most minerals are made from combinations of chemical elements, but a few elements, such as silver (shown here in a rare crystal form), occur naturally by themselves. These are known as native elements and occur in igneous and metamorphic rocks. Some native elements may survive erosion and end up on stream beds.

SILICATES (*see* pp.56–59)
Silicates are metals combined with silicon and oxygen and are the most common minerals. There are more of them than all the other minerals put together. Quartz and feldspar make up the bulk of silicate-rich igneous rock. Other silicate groups include mica, pyroxene, and garnet (shown embedded in a host rock).

OXIDES (*see* pp.62–63)
Oxides, like the chromite shown here, are a combination of a metal with oxygen. They include dull ores, such as bauxite, and rare gems, such as rubies and sapphires. Hard, primary oxides form deep in Earth's crust. Softer oxides form nearer the surface from sulphides and silicates that have broken down.

SULPHIDES (*see* pp.64–65)
Sulphides, like the stibnite shown here, are generally brittle, heavy compounds of sulphur usually combined with a metal. They form as very hot water evaporates underground. They include some important metal ores such as chalcopyrite (a copper ore), cinnabar (a mercury ore), and pyrite (an iron ore).

SULPHATES (*see* pp.66–67)
Sulphates are a large and widespread group of minerals that are generally soft, pale-coloured, and translucent. They form when metals combine with sulphur and oxygen. They include barite and gypsum, shown here in its "daisy" form. Like a daisy, its crystal "petals" radiate outwards from a central point.

CRYSTAL SHAPE ►
All but a few minerals form crystals, and each mineral forms its own characteristic crystal shape, like this tourmaline crystal. Tourmaline crystals are typically long, striped, hexagonal rods. Crystals that form at the same time as the rock in which they are embedded are so small and so mixed in that their characteristic shapes can be hard to spot. In places where crystals have room to grow freely, their characteristic shapes are much clearer.

Tourmaline crystals are usually trigonal and form in many colours

Feldspar is a silicate

Stalactites made of travertine rock form on the overhang of rock terraces

Amethyst crystals fill the inside of this geode

Agate often grows in cracks in lava flows or seabed limestones

Pillow-like formations give Pamukkale ("Cotton Castle") its name

minerals

SPECTACULAR CRYSTALS ▲
Large, well-defined crystals are quite rare and often grow in rock cavities, known as geodes, and veins, where mineral-rich water cools slowly. When the minerals are concentrated and crystals have enough space to grow in regular shapes, they may form valuable gems and spectacular crystals, such as the amethyst and agate shown here. A slow-forming single crystal can grow very big but most crystals form quickly and remain small.

HALIDES (*see* pp.68–69)
Halides are usually very soft minerals, in which metallic elements combine with halogen elements (chlorine, bromine, fluorine, and iodine). Sodium chloride, or table salt, is the best known. Halides dissolve easily in water, so they can only form under special conditions. The most common are halite (salt) and fluorite.

CARBONATES (*see* p.70)
Carbonates are minerals that form when metals or semi-metals combine with a carbonate (carbon and oxygen). Most are formed by the alteration of other minerals on the Earth's surface. Calcite, or calcium carbonate, shown here in its "nailhead" form, makes up the bulk of limestones and marbles.

PHOSPHATES (*see* p.71)
Phosphates are one of the smaller, less common families of minerals. They are usually secondary minerals that form when primary ore minerals are broken down by the weather. When combined with other minerals they often have vivid colours, such as the greenish-blue of turquoise or this lime-green pyromorphite.

MINERALOIDS

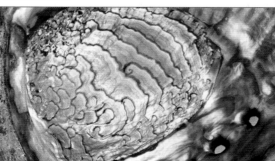

A few substances occur naturally in the Earth and do not fit in with the basic properties of other minerals. They are not members of any of the chemical families (shown left), nor do they form crystals. Such substances are called mineraloids. Some are glassy, like opal and jet (a dense form of coal). Some are formed by living things, such as amber (formed from pine-tree resin) and mother-of-pearl (shown here) which is formed in the shells of certain shellfish.

PHYSICAL PROPERTIES

Although every mineral has a unique combination of features, all share physical properties that help geologists to identify them. They can be grouped according to their habit (how their crystals form); crystal system (the symmetry of their crystal shapes); chemical composition; cleavage (how they split); specific gravity (their density in relation to water); and hardness (how easily they scratch).

ACICULAR
(SOLECITE)

RENIFORM
(HEMATITE)

PRISMATIC
(ORTHOCLASE)

DENDRITIC
(PYROLUSITE)

MASSIVE
(LIMONITE)

BOTRYOIDAL
(HYDROZINCITE)

▲ CRYSTAL HABITS

Crystal habit describes the shapes that minerals form when they grow. Although most minerals have more than one habit, habits are sometimes quite distinctive and common to only a few minerals. The examples shown above are just a small selection of the many different kinds of habit. Acicular crystals form needles; reniform crystals are kidney-shaped; prismatic crystals are symmetrical (one side mirrors the other); dendritic crystals are plant-shaped; and botryoidal crystals look like bunches of grapes. Massive habits have no visible crystals.

CHEMICAL PROPERTIES

Every mineral is a chemical with its own chemical properties. Mineralogists can identify a mineral by its chemistry by putting it in substances, such as acids or water, to see if it dissolves. Although most minerals will not dissolve in pure water, borax and halite are among the exceptions. But many minerals dissolve in acids, especially hot acids. Calcite, for instance, dissolves in weak hydrochloric acid, which helps to distinguish it from similar-looking quartz, which does not dissolve in the acid.

Dissolving calcite fizzes in weak hydrochloric acid

CRYSTAL SYSTEMS

CUBIC
Minerals are classified into six systems according to the symmetrical arrangement of their planes (flat surfaces). Minerals in the cubic system have the most regular crystal symmetry. These include halite (shown here), galena, and silver.

TETRAGONAL
The tetragonal system is one of the least common. Tetragonal crystals typically come as elongated four-sided prisms (a set of parallel faces), shown right. Minerals include chalcopyrite, rutile, scheelite, zircon, and vesuvianite (or idocrase), shown left.

MONOCLINIC
Almost a third of all minerals belong to the monoclinic system, the commonest type of symmetry. Monoclinic crystals are only symmetrical in one plane (shown right). Monoclinic minerals include manganite (shown left), mica, gypsum, and selenite.

TRICLINIC
The least symmetrical crystals are found in the triclinic system. They are also the rarest. Minerals with triclinic systems include anorthite, serpentine, turquoise, kaolinite, and kyanite. Axinite (shown here) gets its name from its distinctive wedge-shaped crystals.

ORTHORHOMBIC
These crystals are quite common. They are short and stubby and generally appear prism or matchbox-shaped (shown right). Minerals in this system include aragonite, sulphur, olivine, topaz, peridot, celestine, adamite, cerussite, and barite (shown left).

HEXAGONAL/TRIGONAL
These two systems are grouped together because they have a similar symmetry. Hexagonal crystals have six faces in the prism (shown right), trigonal crystals have three. Quartz, the gemstone beryl (hexagonal, shown left), and tourmaline all fall into this system.

▲ CLEAVAGE
The way that a mineral breaks along well-defined planes of weakness is called cleavage. Many minerals can be identified by the way they break. Muscovite, shown here, cleaves (splits) cleanly in one direction, forming flat sheets. Fluorite splits in four directions to form diamond-shaped pieces.

▲ CONCHOIDAL FRACTURE
Not all minerals break cleanly along flat cleavage planes. Some show a distinctive way of fracturing. There are about 12 common fracture patterns. One of the most recognizable is the conchoidal, or shell-like shape, where the mineral breaks into curved flakes. Opal (shown here), flint, and obsidian all fracture in this way.

▲ UNEVEN FRACTURE
Striking a mineral with a hammer and breaking it sometimes reveals a rough, uneven surface. Arsenopyrite, pyrite, quartz, kaolinite, anhydrite, and sillimanite (shown here) all fracture unevenly. If the broken surface has sharp edges, geologists call it a jagged fracture.

physical properties

SPECIFIC GRAVITY ▶
Minerals vary in density. Galena, which is rich in lead, is very dense and much heavier than a lump of gypsum the same size. Mineral density can be compared by measuring its specific gravity. This can be a useful clue to identity. A mineral's specific gravity is its weight in relation to the same volume of water. Galena has a specific gravity of 7.5, which means that a lump of galena weighs 7.5 times as much as the same volume of water. Quartz is one of the lighter minerals, with a specific gravity of just 2.65.

Quartz, a silicate, is relatively light

Galena, a sulphide, is very dense

MOHS'S HARDNESS SCALE ▶
Hardness is a mineral's resistance to scratching. It can be measured on a scale that was devised by German mineralogist Friedrich Mohs in 1822. He selected ten standard minerals against which all minerals could be compared. A mineral's position on Mohs's scale depends on whether it can scratch, or be scratched by, Mohs's chosen minerals.

1 TALC	2 GYPSUM	3 CALCITE	4 FLUORITE	5 APATITE	6 ORTHOCLASE	7 QUARTZ	8 TOPAZ	9 CORUNDUM	10 DIAMOND
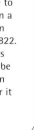		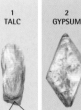			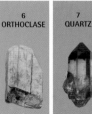				

TALCUM POWDER ▶
The softest mineral on Mohs's hardness scale is talc. Every mineral can scratch talc. Its softness has made it a popular mineral for carving since ancient times. The Chinese, Babylonians, Egyptians, and Native Americans all carved ornaments from talc.

Talcum powder is made from talc

DIAMOND PARTICLES ▶
The hardest mineral on Mohs's hardness scale is diamond. Diamond is so hard that it will scratch every other mineral – and yet cannot be scratched itself. Besides being highly valued as gemstones, diamonds are also in demand in cutting tools and drills.

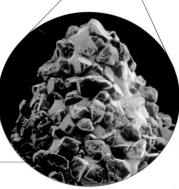

Diamond particles on the tip of a dental drill

OPTICAL PROPERTIES

One of the first clues to a mineral's identity is often the way it looks. Minerals reflect and let light through in different ways. For example, many minerals glint and sparkle, while others barely reflect light at all. Some minerals look greasy, as if they were coated with butter. Some have a distinctive colour. Qualities like these are known as optical properties. Colour, lustre, and clarity are the most obvious, but there are others, including fluorescence and refraction.

Shiny azurite set in dull limonite

LUSTRE ►
Lustre is the way that light bounces off a mineral's surface. A surface can be as shiny as glass or as dull as soil. Here, bright-blue azurite is instantly distinguishable from the brown limonite in which it is set, not just by colour but also by its distinctive glass-like lustre. Some minerals can also be distinguished by the way that light bounces around inside it. For example, when light hits an opal, its chemical structure makes it appear to shimmer with the colours of the rainbow.

Tiny malachite crystals form a crust

◄ COLOUR
Minerals get their colour from their chemical make-up. Some minerals, such as cuprite (a mixture of copper and oxygen, shown here), are coloured by the main chemicals in their make-up and always appear the same colour. Minerals like these are known as idiochromatic. Other minerals, such as quartz, vary wildly in colour. They get their colouring from impurities and are known as allochromatic minerals. Quartz takes its many different colours from trace minerals; rose quartz is pink due to traces of titanium, while chrysoprase is green because of traces of nickel.

Uneven, submetallic lustre

DIFFERENT COLOURS

CITRINE
Yellow, orange, or brown citrine is a variety of quartz – an allochromatic mineral. Its colours are caused by minute traces of iron. Pale yellow citrine stones are the most highly prized and give the mineral its name, after the Latin word "citrus" for lemon. Heating citrine turns it white.

AMETHYST
Like citrine, amethyst is another variety of quartz that gets its colouring from tiny traces of iron. However, because amethyst forms at lower temperatures, it appears purple. If heated, it turns yellow, while exposure to X-rays restores its original colour. The best quality amethysts are found in geodes (rock hollows).

AZURITE
Azurite, an idiochromatic mineral, has a distinctive bright blue colour. It is the most common blue mineral and its name comes from the French word "azure", meaning 'blue sky'. It is made of a mixture of copper, carbonate, and hydrogen. Painters ground it up to make a vivid blue pigment that was almost as good as lapis lazuli.

STREAK TESTS

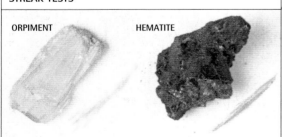

ORPIMENT   HEMATITE

A mineral's streak is the mark it leaves when it is dragged across a ceramic tile. Some minerals, such as orpiment (shown above), are the same colour as their streak, while others produce a streak of different colour. Their streaks help to tell them apart. Hematite (shown above) and chromite both look black, but chromite's streak is black, while hematite's is brownish red. Minerals, such as fluorite, appear in many colours but have the same coloured streak. Flourite's is always white.

TYPES OF LUSTRE

VITREOUS (GLASSY)
The word vitreous comes from the Latin word for "jelly" and describes the texture of an eye. Mineralogists use it to mean a shiny, glass-like lustre. Most clear and semi-transparent gems are characterized by a vitreous lustre, including ruby (shown here), topaz, emerald, tourmaline, aquamarine, corundum, and fluorite.

METALLIC
A metallic lustre is a shiny, highly reflective finish that is typical of freshly cut metals and their ores. All native metals have this lustre when newly broken or polished. So too do many ores, such as galena, chalcopyrite, pyrite, and magnetite. Graphite (shown here) is not a metal but has a dull metallic lustre.

SUBMETALLIC
Some minerals have what is called a submetallic lustre. This is an uneven, semi-metallic reflection from the mineral's surface – caused by traces of metal in the mineral. It is often seen on dark, almost opaque (non-transparent) crystals, such as chromite, cuprite, rutile, sphalerite, and lepidocrocite (shown here).

GREASY
Minerals with a greasy lustre have an oily appearance. Although they are shiny, they do not show reflections like glass. This kind of lustre is common in minerals with microscopically small amounts of mineral impurities. Halite (shown here), quartz, and apatite all have a greasy appearance.

SILKY
Minerals with a silky lustre tend to have a fine structure of fibres that makes them shimmer, just like silk. Fibrous asbestos minerals, such as serpentine chrysotile and riebeckite crocidolite all have a silky lustre. So do minerals, such as gypsum (shown here), wavellite, tremolite, and fibrous calcite.

optical properties

Azurite crystals have a glassy lustre

◄ FLUORESCENCE
When some minerals are exposed to ultraviolet light, they glow in colours that are different from their normal colour in daylight. This glow is called fluorescence – a word that comes from the mineral fluorite (shown here), which comes in many colours but which gives off a blue or green fluorescence. Fluorite is thought to fluoresce because it contains minute amounts of uranium or "rare earth" elements – a group of chemically similar metals. Sometimes fluorescence is caused by tiny impurities in minerals. For example, traces of manganese give calcite a bright-red glow.

Fluorite glows bright blue in ultraviolet light

OPAQUE: GOLD **TRANSLUCENT: AQUAMARINE**

▲ CLARITY
A few minerals, such as quartz and sapphire are almost as transparent (clear) as glass in their pure state. However, tiny impurities can make them appear less clear. Some minerals, such as moonstone, are semi-transparent, so that things seen through them appear blurred. Geologists describe minerals that are not transparent, but which still let some light through them, such as chrysoprase, as translucent. Minerals that block off light completely, such as malachite, are said to be opaque. All metals are opaque.

Calcite distorts light

REFRACTION ►
Some minerals are very clear and transparent but distort the light passing through them. They are said to refract (bend) the light. For example, objects seen through calcite appear twice due to double refraction. The light reflected off this black line is split into two rays, which produce a double image.

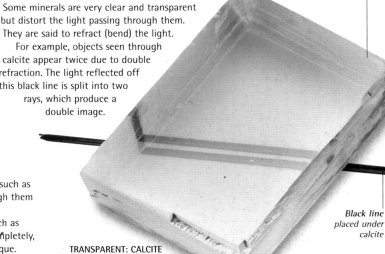

Black line placed under calcite

TRANSPARENT: CALCITE

NATIVE ELEMENTS

Most minerals are compounds, which means they are made up of combinations of chemical elements. But some minerals occur naturally by themselves, and these are called native elements. They are often metals, but also include semi-metals, such as bismuth, antimony, and arsenic, and non-metals, such as sulphur and carbon (in the form of graphite and diamond). Non-metals are usually found in volcanic features such as underground veins and – with sulphur – in hot springs. Sulphur and graphite are common, but bismuth, antimony, and arsenic occur rarely as native elements – and diamonds are rarest of all.

Chunky orthorhombic crystals

Needle-like monoclinic crystals

▲ TWO HABITS OF SULPHUR
Chunky orthorhombic crystals (*see* p46) are the most common form of sulphur. Occasionally, though, it is found in monoclinic form (*see* p46). Monoclinic sulphur can be the same vivid yellow as ordinary sulphur – though it is more often orange – but the crystals are acicular, which means they are long and needle-like.

Cloth provides some protection from the poisonous sulphur gases

Sulphur deposits found near volcanic hot springs

▲ SULPHUR MINING
Native sulphur is recognizable by its bright yellow colour. It is often found around the edges of hot volcanic springs and smoky volcanic chimneys called fumaroles. Here, a miner is digging sulphur from the crater of Ijen volcano in eastern Java, Indonesia. In this type of sulphur mining, people collect chunks of cooled sulphur from around the crater and carry them away in baskets. Most of the world's sulphur, however, is mined from underground beds, such as those found under the Gulf of Mexico, using the Frasch process in which very hot water, injected into the beds at very high pressure, melts the sulphur. The molten sulphur is then pumped to the surface. After the water evaporates, pure sulphur is left behind.

◄ PROCESSING SULPHUR
While nearly pure sulphur can be extracted from the ground using the Frasch process, sulphur is also found in fossil fuels and ores such as pyrite and galena. In these cases, the sulphur is separated out by heating the mineral to release hydrogen sulphide gas. The gas is then burned to separate the hydrogen off, leaving pure sulphur. Most commercially extracted sulphur is turned into sulphuric acid in large chemical plants, such as the one in England shown here. Sulphuric acid has many uses in industry. It is used to make fertilizer, dyes, paper, and cellophane.

▲ GRAPHITE
Graphite and diamond are both forms of carbon, but the two could hardly be more different. Graphite is opaque, dark grey, and one of the softest minerals – so soft it is used as the "lead" in pencils. More recently, scientists have produced a man-made form of graphite called graphene, which may be used in the future, instead of silicon, for ultra-fast computer chips. Most graphite forms in rocks (usually marble) through the metamorphism of organic material, such as fossils.

▲ DIAMOND
The world's hardest natural substance, diamond is pure carbon that has been transformed into a clear, hard gemstone by incredible forces of pressure and heat. Most diamonds found today are billions of years old. They formed deep underground and were carried to the surface through volcanic pipes in molten kimberlite magma. They survived because they are so hard. Pressure like this is rare in nature.

GRAPHITE AND DIAMOND CHEMICAL STRUCTURES

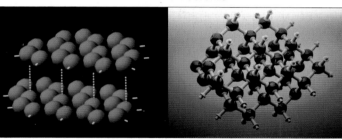

Pure carbon occurs in four forms: graphite, diamond, soot (burnt organic matter), and a very rare form called fullerene. In graphite, the atoms form in two-dimensional, sheet-like structures (above left). However, the bonds between the sheets are weak, which is why graphite is so soft. In the diamond form, the atoms are bonded into a strong, three-dimensional framework (above right). This is why diamond is so hard.

native elements

Dull, non-metallic sheen

Botryoidal (grape-like) clusters

▲ ANTIMONY
Although silvery-grey like a metal, antimony is called a semi-metal because it sometimes behaves chemically like a metal, sometimes like a non-metal. Antimony occurs rarely as a native element – usually in volcanic veins. The main source of antimony is stibnite, a sulphide ore. Ancient Egyptians used it for eyeliner, and medieval artists used it for painting.

▲ BISMUTH
Bismuth is found as a native element only rarely, mostly in volcanic veins. Like antimony, it is a semi-metal and expands on freezing as water does. This property makes bismuth very useful for soldering metals together because it expands to fill any gap as it solidifies. Bismuth is usually extracted from the ores bismuthinite and bismite.

▲ ARSENIC
Sometimes, pure arsenic forms botryoidal (grape-like) clusters, such as those shown here. However, arsenic is usually found combined in minerals such as arsenopyrite, orpiment, and realgar. Pure arsenic is poisonous. It can be combined with other minerals in making many things, from electronic transistors to wood preservatives.

METAL ELEMENTS

A few of the less reactive metals, including gold, silver, platinum, and copper, can be found in pure form as metal elements. Nuggets or flakes of these metals can be taken straight from rock, but this is uncommon. In the crust, most of Earth's metals are found mixed up with other elements in ores. Gold, almost uniquely, is mainly found as a native element. Metal elements are quite rare in the Earth's crust, but they are more common in the core. Most of Earth's iron, for example, sank to the core very early in Earth's history, because it was so heavy.

Gold in quartz

▲ GOLD

Gold is the least reactive of all metals; it stays uncorroded (not damaged by chemical action) and shiny almost indefinitely. It was one of the first metals to be used because it was found in the ground in pure form, glittering in cracks and on the surface of rocks. It is also soft enough to hammer easily into shape. Many of the world's most beautiful ancient artefacts are made from gold. They have survived unblemished by time.

SILVER ►

Silver was known as "white gold" by the Ancient Egyptians and was once more highly prized than gold. It was first used in Anatolia, Turkey, more than 5,000 years ago. When polished, it is a beautiful, shiny white metal, but exposure to air quickly tarnishes it with a black coat of silver sulphide. This coating makes it hard to spot in the ground. Like gold, it forms in volcanic veins, often with galena (lead ore), zinc, and copper. Unlike gold and platinum, it rarely forms nuggets. Today, silver is mainly used for tableware and in many electrical components, because it conducts electricity very well, even better than copper.

SILVER ORE

TARNISHED SILVER

Copper wire coiled up on drums

◄ COPPER

Copper's distinctive reddish colour makes it the most instantly recognizable of all metals. It is quite soft and is often found in its native form. Copper was one of the first metals people learned to use, because they could find and extract it easily. Today, most copper is taken from deposits of chalcopyrite ore. Like silver, it often grows in branching dendritic crystals, and like silver, it tarnishes quickly on exposure to air. However, the tarnish on copper is bright green, not black, so copper deposits are often revealed by bright green stains on a rock's surface, known as copper blooms.

Copper blooms are green from oxidization (exposure to the air)

native elements

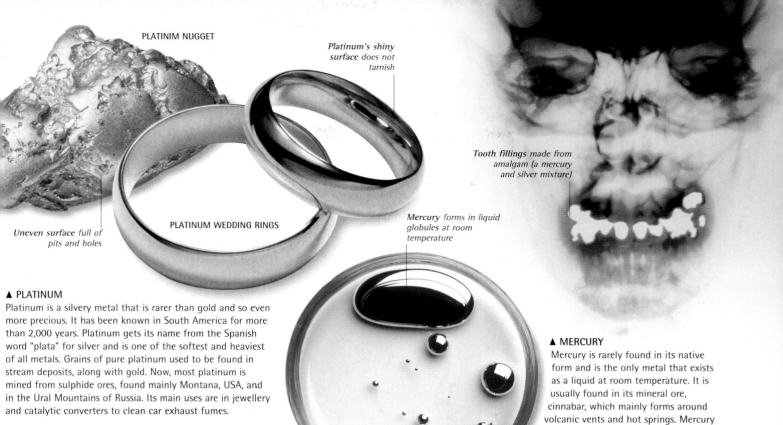

PLATINIM NUGGET

Platinum's shiny surface does not tarnish

PLATINUM WEDDING RINGS

Uneven surface full of pits and holes

Tooth fillings made from amalgam (a mercury and silver mixture)

▲ PLATINUM

Platinum is a silvery metal that is rarer than gold and so even more precious. It has been known in South America for more than 2,000 years. Platinum gets its name from the Spanish word "plata" for silver and is one of the softest and heaviest of all metals. Grains of pure platinum used to be found in stream deposits, along with gold. Now, most platinum is mined from sulphide ores, found mainly Montana, USA, and in the Ural Mountains of Russia. Its main uses are in jewellery and catalytic converters to clean car exhaust fumes.

Mercury forms in liquid globules at room temperature

▲ MERCURY

Mercury is rarely found in its native form and is the only metal that exists as a liquid at room temperature. It is usually found in its mineral ore, cinnabar, which mainly forms around volcanic vents and hot springs. Mercury expands with heat and is best known for its use in thermometers (devices used to measure temperature).

MERCURY

NICKEL-SILVER COMMEMORATIVE COIN

ЧЕМПІОНАТ СВІТУ З ФУТБОЛУ НІМЕЧЧИНА 2006

Lead covering on roof helps to protect it against the weather

NICKEL ORE

▲ NICKEL–IRON

Less common than some major elements, nickel forms a natural alloy with iron, called nickel-iron, which is often found in meteorites on Earth's surface. The Ancient Egyptians called it "sky-iron" and used it to make the sacred tools for mummifying pharaohs. Today, nickel is mostly used in alloys with iron and other metals to make stainless steel and with silver to make coins. Both nickel and iron are produced mainly from ores: pentlandite for nickel, and hematite and magnetite for iron.

▲ LEAD

Lead is a very dark, soft metal. Its softness makes it easy to use and shape – which is why the Ancient Romans used it to make water pipes. Lead is also very heavy – one of the densest of all metals. It is rarely found as a native element. More often it is combined with other elements, in galena, anglesite, and cerussite. In fact, even lead pipes are not made from pure lead. Because the metal is so soft, it is usually alloyed (mixed) with other elements.

NATIVE LEAD (GREY) IN ROCK

Gold is a native element, prized for its bright yellow colour and resistance to tarnishing. Gold deposits typically form in two ways. Most gold is formed in hydrothermal veins in the rock, where it appears mixed in with quartz and other minerals (such as silver and sulphides). Most of the world's gold is mined from veins like these. Gold is also found in deposits in riverbeds, where gold grains from weathered rock accumulate.

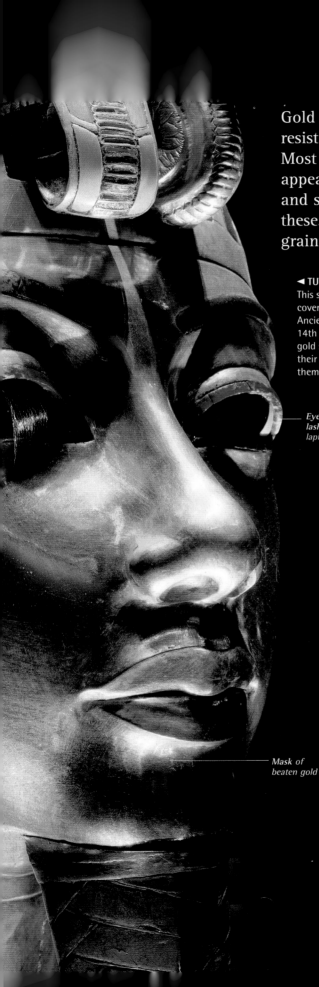

◄ **TUTANKHAMUN'S FUNERAL MASK**
This stunning gold funeral mask was found covering the mummy of Tutankhamun, an Ancient Egyptian boy-king. He lived in the 14th century BC. For the Ancient Egyptians, gold symbolized everlasting life, so they packed their pharaohs' tombs with gold objects for them to use in the afterlife.

Eyebrows and lashes made from lapis lazuli

Rare large nugget

GOLD NUGGET ◄
Gold is usually found in branches of tir crystals covering quartz, or in sma grains. Large nuggets are quite rare. Th largest nugget ever found was th famous 71-kg (157-lb) "Welcom Stranger Nugget" found in 186 in Moliagul, Australi

Rare cubic crystals

◄ **GOLD CRYSTALS**
Gold crystals are typically cubic, but unlike many other minerals, gold rarely forms crystals. When they do occur, they are often distorted or microscopic. The finest specimens found since ancient times have usually been melted down for use. So crystal growths like the one shown here are treasured and worth much more than their weight in gold.

Mask of beaten gold

USES OF GOLD

MONEY
Gold has always played a major role in nations' economies. Many of the earliest coins were gold. But gold is rare, expensive, and heavy. Today, its main monetary use is in the gold bars that make up a nation's gold reserves. The largest of these belongs to the USA, followed by Germany.

TEETH
Gold is highly resistant to corrosion. The Etruscans of ancient Italy used gold wire to secure false teeth 2,700 years ago. Since then, gold has been widely used in dentistry, for filling, crowning, or even replacing teeth. It is often alloyed with palladium, silver, zinc, or copper to make it tougher.

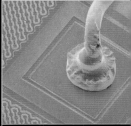

ELECTRONIC CONTACTS
Gold is almost as effective at conducting electricity as copper and silver. Gold-plated connectors and gold wires (shown here) are widely used in electronics, featuring in everything from mobile phones to computers. In 2001, 200 tonnes (197 tons) of gold were used worldwide in electronic components.

around in a pan to
reveal grains of gold

In the 19th century, the discovery of gold deposits anywhere in the world inspired hordes of prospectors to descend on the spot in the hope of striking it rich. There were many gold rushes in North America, the most famous of which was the California gold rush of 1849. Here, prospectors use a home-made sluice to wash away silt in the hope of finding gold grains. There was only enough gold to make a few lucky people rich – most prospectors found little or nothing.

◄ PANNING FOR GOLD

When rock containing gold is broken down by the weather, gold grains may be washed into streams or rivers. Gold is quite dense so the grains accumulate in deposits on riverbeds. Recovering these grains involves a labour-intensive technique known as panning. This involves scooping shingle from the riverbed into a pan, then carefully swilling the water around until the lighter gravels are rinsed out, leaving the heavier gold grains behind.

OPENCAST MINING ►

Estimates suggest that all the gold ever mined amounts to around 145,000 tonnes (142,700 tons) and that a further 2,500 tonnes (2,460 tons) or so are dug up each year. In the past, most of this gold came from South Africa. Extracting the gold here means digging expensive, ever-deeper mines. More recently, gold-mining companies have begun to exploit deposits nearer the surface in places such as Indonesia, Russia, Australia, and Papua New Guinea (shown here). Gold can be extracted more cheaply from opencast mines, which are large pits in the ground. But their wide-scale excavation poses much more of a threat to the environment.

e ►►

gold

Excavators used for
digging in opencast mine

Gold ore excavated
from terraces

PYRITE (FOOL'S GOLD)

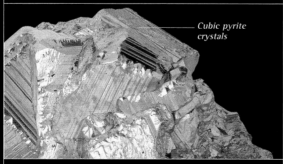

Cubic pyrite
crystals

The shiny, yellow mineral called pyrite (an iron sulphide) looks so much like gold that it has fooled many prospectors into thinking they have found the real thing. Yet pyrite, sometimes known as "fool's gold", is among the commonest minerals and is found in most environments. Indeed, any rock that looks a little rusty probably contains pyrite. Its crystals form in a number of shapes, including cubes and pentagonal dodecahedrons, which have 12 five-sided faces.

UNDERGROUND MINING ►

To extract gold from the ground, gold-containing ores have to be dug from the surface or out of underground seams. The gold is then separated from the waste ore in a process known as flotation, smelted (a combination of heating and melting), and then refined into 99.5 per cent pure gold. This geologist is taking a sample from deep below the surface. Analysis of the sample for gold content will determine whether it is worth continuing to mine.

FELSIC SILICATES

Silicates make up more than 90 per cent of the weight of Earth's crust, and most rocks are mainly composed of them. There are more than 1,000 different silicate minerals, split into two types: felsic and mafic silicates. Silicates that form in granites are called felsic silicates. The word felsic is a combination of "fel" for feldspar and "sic" for silica. They are lighter in weight and colour than other silicates, because they contain less iron and magnesium. The felsic silicates include quartz (pure silica) and the K-feldspars, which are rich in potassium (K). Micas are a group of silicate minerals that split easily into sheets.

Debris from erosion

Volcanic plug exposed after erosion

POTASSIUM (K-) FELDSPARS

ORTHOCLASE
Orthoclase is an important rock-forming mineral. Orthoclase and plagioclase (*see* p.58) feldspar, make up 60 per cent of the Earth's crust. Orthoclase is one of the main minerals in granite rock, along with mica and quartz. When granite erodes, the orthoclase is recycled in arkose (feldspar-rich) sandstones.

SANIDINE
Sanidine (shown here) forms in a variety of volcanic rocks, such as trachyte and rhyolite, and in contact metamorphic rocks, such as marble and hornfels. It is usually colourless or white, with a white streak. It can form in massive or prismatic (shown here) habits (*see* p46). The crystals are often twinned (*see* p59).

ANORTHOCLASE
Anorthoclase is a K-feldspar similar to sanidine and another K-feldspar called albite. However, unlike them, it is rich in both sodium and potassium. Sanidine contains little sodium, and albite contains very little potassium. Anorthoclase generally forms in igneous rocks in dykes and small intrusions.

silicates

BOARS TUSK VOLCANIC PLUG ▲
Boars Tusk in Wyoming, USA, is the core of an ancient volcano. Over millions of years, the softer external rock has worn away, exposing the tougher rock that plugged the volcano's vent. This rock is rhyolite – similar to granite, but formed near the surface, rather than deep underground. The rocks have the same felsic minerals – quartz, potassium feldspar, and mica – but granite can contain microcline or orthoclase (potassium), while rhyolite contains sanidine (potassium and sodium).

MICROCLINE AND PORCELAIN ▶
Microcline is the main K-feldspar found in igneous and metamorphic rocks, forming at relatively low temperatures in deep rocks, such as syenite and pegmatite. Microcline crystals in pegmatite are the largest ever found. A specimen from Karelia, Russia, weighed more than 2,030 tonnes (2,000 tons). The Chinese used microcline to make fine porcelain more than 1,500 years ago. When heated, tiny microcline particles help to cement the finely ground kaolin ("white clay") and quartz together into a white, translucent ceramic.

Glaze (a hard, water-resistant coating) also made from microcline

CHINESE PORCELAIN VASE

Amazonite is a gemstone variety of green microcline

Clear muscovite sheet used as window pane

MICAS

MUSCOVITE
Muscovite looks brittle but is remarkably tough. It is often found in sands where other minerals have been destroyed. In Muscovy (old Russia) it was used for house windows, giving it its name. Its heat-resistant qualities meant that it was once used in stove windows. Today, it is used for making electrical components.

BIOTITE
Biotite mica is a common mineral and a major ingredient in granites, gneisses, and schists. It is darker than muscovite – usually black or dark brown – and is soft and crumbles easily. Flakes of biotite often stick together in clumps up to 2 m (7 ft) in diameter. These clumps are known as "books", because they resemble pages.

LEPIDOLITE
Lepidolite is a rare mica, forming in thin flakes in acid igneous rocks, such as granite. Its pink, purple, or grey colouring comes from the presence of the metal lithium. It often forms together with tourmaline – the combination of pink lepidolite and red tourmaline is attractive in carved ornaments.

▲ MICA WINDOW
Mica minerals are found in all kinds of rock. In some pegmatites, they typically form thin, colourless, brittle flakes. Some micas, such as muscovite, are extremely clear and resistant to weathering. As a result, the sheets of mica were once used as window panes, like this one from a Native American dwelling situated high on a rock outcrop in Acoma Pueblo, New Mexico, USA. Mica has heat-resistant properties and is still used in oil stoves and lamps.

Pinky purple tourmaline is called rubellite

◄ TOURMALINE
Tourmaline minerals occur in a wide range of vivid colours. Quite often, single long crystals have multi-coloured layers, like an exotic cocktail. Each layer reflects a slight chemical change during its formation. Red tourmaline becomes electrically charged on heating.

TOURMALINE

Quartz matrix

Beryl turned to green emerald by impurities

Quartz vein containing emeralds

Emeralds will be prised out of the rock by hand to avoid damage

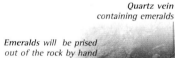

BERYL ►
Beryl is a widespread mineral. Pure beryl (goshenite) is colourless, but impurities give it rich colours. When chrome and vanadium turn it to brilliant green, as shown here, it becomes an emerald. Blue beryl is called aquamarine, yellow beryl is called heliodor, and pink beryl is called morganite. Beryl is an important source of beryllium, which is used in nuclear reactors and for making metal alloys.

EMERALD

EMERALD MINING ►
Beryl is found most commonly in pegmatites where it forms gigantic crystals. Archaeological excavations show that it has been mined for thousands of years. In 1816, the French explorer Cailliaud discovered Ancient Egyptian beryl mines dating back to 1650 BC. Other discoveries from the Red Sea reveal mines dating back to the time of Queen Cleopatra. The finest emeralds come from South America, especially Chivor and Muzo in Colombia (shown here).

MAFIC SILICATES

The family of silicates known as mafic silicates get their name from a combination of "Ma" for magnesium, and "fic" for iron (from ferric). They typically form in magmas that well up where tectonic plates are pulling apart, such as under the ocean floor, and make up the building blocks of the basic group of igneous rocks (*see* p.27), which includes basalt and gabbro. The mafic silicate minerals olivine and pyroxene, found in basic and ultrabasic rocks, are denser and darker than felsic silicates. Other mafic silicates, called plagioclase feldspars, are characterized by varying proportions of calcium and sodium in their chemical structure.

PLAGIOCLASE FELDSPARS

OLIGOCLASE
Each variety of plagioclase feldspar has a different proportion of sodium or calcium. Oligoclase is a white or yellow mineral that contains more sodium than calcium. In its gem form, it is known as moonstone or sunstone if it has traces of hematite.

ANORTHITE
The plagioclase feldspar with the least sodium and the most calcium is anorthite. This causes the crystal to refract or bend light in a different way than other plagioclase feldspars. In fact, each of the plagioclases can be identified by the way it refracts light.

PERIDOT

◄ OLIVINE
Instantly recognizable due to their dark-green colour, olivines are rich in iron and magnesium. In some places, such as Hawaii (shown left), olivine grains can turn river and beach sands green. Olivines are very common in mafic rocks such as basalt and gabbro. The group of igneous rocks known as ultramafic include peridotite and dunite and are almost pure olivine. Since most of the Earth's mantle is made from olivine peridotite, olivine may be the most common mineral in the Earth. However, in the crust it is much less common and rarely occurs larger than microscopic grains. This is the reason why large, green gem crystals called peridots are so highly prized.

Sand contains green olivine grains

ANORTHOSITE ►
Richer in plagioclase feldspar than any other rock – almost 100 per cent – anorthosite is closely related to diorite and gabbro. The plagioclase feldspar in anorthosite rock is typically rich in calcium. It is found in a few 1.5-billion-year-old outcrops on the Earth, including the Appalachian Mountains, USA, and in southern Scandinavia. But the Highlands of the Moon and the planet Mercury are thought to be largely made of anorthosite rock. The Apollo 16 Mission brought back four-billion-year-old chunks of this rock from the Moon.

Samples of anorthosite rock from the Moon

Anorthosite rock is very light and floated to the surface when the Moon was molten

AUGITE

Rare large crystal

ACTINOLITE

▲ PYROXENES

Among the most common rock-forming minerals are pyroxenes, such as augite (shown here) and diopside. They form stubby, dark-green crystals. Pyroxenes are found in most igneous and metamorphic rocks. Darker mafic rocks, such as gabbro and basalt, contain lots of pyroxene. Pyroxenes form when there is little water present in the rocks. Pyroxene comes from the Greek words for "fire" and "stranger", because mineralogists were surprised to see these dark green crystals in hot lava.

▲ AMPHIBOLES

Like pyroxenes, amphiboles, such as actinolite (shown here) and hornblende, are common rock-forming silicates, rich in iron and magnesium. However, unlike pyroxenes, they form at lower temperatures with water present, and often grow into blade-like or thread-like masses of crystals. Tremolite is whitish-grey and contains calcium, magnesium, and some iron. Green nephrite (a source of jade) combines actinolite and tremolite. Amphibole cleavage meets in a diamond shape, while pyroxene cleavage meets at right angles.

METAMORPHIC

Like most minerals, silicates can be changed by heat and pressure as rocks become metamorphosed. Mild metamorphism changes silicates to hydrous minerals. These are minerals, such as serpentine and chlorite, that contain water. Intense metamorphism dries the silicates out, initially creating minerals such as muscovite and biotite, followed by garnets.

Red garnet crystals can be seen in this sample of eclogite

silicates

Silicate containing aluminium and iron

STAUROLITE

▲ STAUROLITE CROSS

One of the most amazing examples of twinning is provided by staurolite, which forms in metamorphic rock. Here, two crystals interpenetrate so completely that it looks as if they grew out of each other. In the highly prized variant shown here, the crystals grow at right angles, giving the mineral its name – from the Greek word for cross. Its resemblance to the Maltese cross – the symbol with four arms of equal length adopted by the crusading Knights of St John – gives the mineral its Christian association and reputation as a good luck charm. In another variety of staurolite, the crystals cross at 60°.

TWINNING

PLAGIOCLASE
Crystals of plagioclase feldspars, such as albite (shown here), are renowned for their "twinning". Twinning is caused by an error during crystallization. Instead of a normal single crystal, the crystals double and seem to grow out of each other like Siamese twins. Twinning follows rules called twin laws.

SPHENE (TITANITE)
There are two kinds of twinning: contact and penetration. Contact twins, like those in sphene (shown here) have a distinct boundary between the two crystals, so they look like mirror images of each other. Penetration twin crystals, like those in neptunite and phenakite, appear to grow right across each other.

LABRADORITE
Twinning is not always seen on the surface. In labradorite, the twinning occurs in sheets inside the mineral. This affects the way that light travels through the crystals, creating a spectacular display of colouring, known as labradorescence. Colours change from blues and violets to greens and oranges.

QUARTZ

Quartz, a silicate, is made up of oxygen and silica. It is very common and is a major ingredient of most igneous and metamorphic rock. Quartz is very tough and does not break down, so it provides much of the raw material for clastic (particle) sedimentary rock, such as sandstone and shale. Although pure quartz is colourless, impurities give it a range of colours and forms. Despite being so common, quartz's range of colours mean that some quartz crystals are valued as semi-precious gems.

MOSS AGATE
CHALCEDONY

GREEN CHRYSOPRASE
CHALCEDONY

▲ CHALCEDONY
When quartz forms at low temperatures in volcanic cavities, the crystals are so tiny that they resemble smooth porcelain. This cryptocrystalline quartz is called chalcedony and comes in an array of colours and patterns, including blood-red carnelian, apple-green chrysoprase, moss agate, and reddish brown sard. The name chalcedony comes from Chalkedon, Turkey, where the mineral was mined in ancient times.

QUARTZ VARIETIES

ROCK CRYSTAL
Rock crystal is the purest quartz, and the chunky six-sided crystals are as clear as ice. Historically, the crystals were shaped to make fortune-tellers' crystal balls or sparkling chandeliers. Rock crystal is now used in making watches, because it has a natural electric charge that helps to regulate the mechanism.

AMETHYST
Traces of ferric (iron) oxide in quartz give amethyst a purple or mauve colour. The name comes from the Greek myth of the maiden Amethyst. When the goddess Artemis turned her into white stone to save her from tigers, Dionysus, the god of wine, poured deep-red wine over her, staining her purple.

MILKY QUARTZ
Quartz crystals can form with things trapped inside. These internal features are called inclusions and can be anything from gas bubbles to insects. Milky quartz contains tiny bubbles of fluid that make it look white. Milky quartz inclusions trapped in other types of quartz are known as "phantoms".

SMOKY QUARTZ
Smoky quartz is a dark brown, transparent gemstone. Other similar varieties include black morion, and black-and-grey coontail quartz. The dark colour comes from exposure to radioactive elements (such as radium) under the ground. Smoky quartz is found in the Swiss Alps and the Cairngorm Mountains in Scotland.

ROSE QUARTZ
Rose quartz gets its pink colour from traces of iron and titanium. Rose quartz is not treated as a gemstone because it does not often form clear crystals. Instead, it is made into ornaments, and jewellery. The Romans carved it into objects used for stamping wax seals. The best specimens of rose quartz are found in Brazil.

Sand dune made up of trillions of quartz grains

▲ SAND DUNES
Quartz never completely disintegrates. Instead, it eventually breaks down into sand-sized grains. Quartz sand accumulates in dry regions on Earth – at least a quarter of the world's deserts are made up of quartz sand. In northern Africa's Sahara Desert, there are 12 or so giant sand fields known as ergs. In western North America, the Great Navajo Erg was formed in the Jurassic period about 150 million years ago. Today, it has turned to rock again and is preserved in the form of sandstone.

BLUE LACE AGATE

Fine-grained blue lace banding

Agate originates in effusive lava, filling gaps left behind by gas bubbles

▲ AGATE

When traces of iron, manganese, and other chemicals create bands in chalcedony, it is known as agate. Moss agate is white chalcedony with mossy bands of green chlorite. Blue lace agate has alternating bands of mauve-blue and white. Onyx has black-and-white bands. Thunder eggs have star-shaped, brown-and-yellow bands. Although the bands form naturally, agate that is sold commercially is often stained by artificial dyes.

HOW AGATE IS FORMED ▲

Agates ususally form in basalt lavas, and agate pebbles can be found in beaches or riverbeds in areas of basalt rock, like here in British Columbia, Canada. Frothy basalt lavas solidify quickly when they flood to the surface, trapping gas bubbles. Water moving through the pile of lavas picks up silica and other elements, such as iron, and deposits them in the bubbles. As the lava cools, the dissolved minerals crystallize inside the bubbles. Coloured bands are created as the chemistry of the water changes over time.

e ▸▸ quartz

SILICON CHIPS

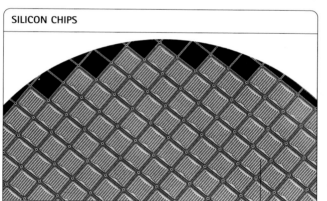

Quartz is a form of silica or silicon dioxide. Silicon is a semi-conductor, which means it can transmit electricity. Today, one of its main uses is to make modern electronic components. Computer microprocessors are made with silicon chips, which were invented in 1958 by an American research scientist, Jack Kilby. These are minute squares of silicon onto which electrical circuits are printed in gold, silver, or copper. The chips are made in large wafers, which are then broken up for use.

Silicon chips are printed in tiny squares on large wafers

Spoil heaps (waste) from opal mine workings cover the landscape

OPAL ▶

Opal does not form crystals and looks more like pearly coloured glass than a traditional mineral. Opals form in different ways as silica-rich fluids solidify – often in hot springs or volcanic rocks. Chemically, opals are a combination of silica and water. Heating opal removes the water molecules and can turn it into quartz. Black opal and fire opal are the most prized varieties. Fire opal, which is coloured red and yellow, is mined in Querétaro, Mexico.

Opalescence is the term for this shimmering of colours

▲ OPAL MINING IN AUSTRALIA

Ninety per cent of the world's opals come from Australia. The first opal field to be exploited was at White Cliffs, New South Wales (shown here), but this is now exhausted. The main field was at the famous Coober Pedy in South Australia. The days are so hot and the nights are so cold here that most people live underground. This earned Coober Pedy its name, which comes from the Aboriginal words for "White Man in a hole".

Sapphire said to have belonged to the 11th-century English king, Edward the Confessor

IMPERIAL STATE CROWN

Spinel (Black Prince's Ruby)

OXIDES

Although 90 per cent of the Earth's minerals contain oxygen, the term oxide is generally used to describe minerals that are a simple combination of a metal with oxygen, or a metal with oxygen and hydrogen (an hydroxide). Oxides form a large group, occurring in most geological environments and rock types. Oxide minerals include everything from common cassiterite (tin ore) to precious gems such as sapphires and rubies (forms of corundum). Oxides vary in colour from rich-red rubies to dull-black iron ores.

HEMATITE HABITS

RENIFORM
Hematite has been mined since ancient times as an iron ore. It forms in a variety of habits (shapes), including reniform (kidney-shaped), shown above. Hematite comes from the Greek word for blood. When powdered, it makes a red colour. According to Greek myth, it formed from blood-stained rocks on battlefields.

MASSIVE
The massive form (no visible crystals) of hematite can be easily weathered and shows a distinctive brownish-red streak, similar to rust. Like rust, this streak is produced when water reacts with iron to produce iron oxide. Small flecks of specular hematite (shiny, reflective crystals) can be seen dotted around the specimen.

SPECULARITE
Specular hematite has grey, metallic, hexagonal-shaped crystals. Lion Cavern in Swaziland, South Africa, is an ancient source of specularite. It is said to be the world's oldest mine, dating back 40,000 years. African bushmen used specularite as a cosmetic. They rubbed it on their heads to make them shimmer.

▲ SPINEL

Spinels are a group of minerals that are made from combinations of metal oxides. The semi-precious gem spine is magnesium aluminium oxide. Traces of other metals give it a variety of colours, including blue, green, purple, and brown, but the typical colour is a red that rivals the red of ruby. Many gems once thought to be rubies have proved to be spinels. The most famous example is the large Black Prince's Ruby, set in the British Imperial State Crown (shown here). The "ruby" was given to Edward the Black Prince (of Wales) in 1366 by Pedro the Cruel of Spain. Gem-quality spinels are still found in Sri Lanka, India, and Thailand.

SPINEL

MAGNETITE ▶

Magnetite is a naturally magnetic iron ore. The word magnet comes from the Ancient Greek town of Magnesia, where large quantities of magnetic iron ore were found. The ancient Chinese were the first to exploit these magnetic properties. Feng shui practitioners use a direction-finding compass to advise people where to position graves or new buildings in order to maximize the flow of "chi" (Earth energy) around them and create a better setting. At first the Chinese used spoons shaped from magnetite to indicate a north-south direction, but later they used magnetized needles, as in the feng shui compass shown here.

Iron needle magnetized by rubbing it with magnetite

Chinese feng shui compass divided into "24 mountains" (15° segments)

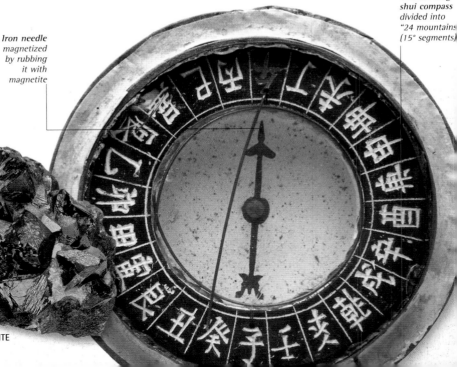

oxides

MAGNETITE

◄ SAPPHIRE

Sapphire is a precious form of corundum, one of the hardest minerals. The blue colour is caused by traces of iron and titanium. Sapphires are often found in river gravels, where they accumulate after the rocks in which they form are broken up. Kashmir, in India, and Australia are famous for their sapphires. Besides jewellery, sapphires are also used in mechanical engineering and for making lasers.

◄ RUBY

Ruby is another precious corundum and is coloured by traces of chromium. The ancient Hindus called it *Rajnapura*, meaning "king of gems". For centuries, the finest rubies came from the Mogok region of Burma, where they formed in marble and other metamorphic rocks. Star rubies (and star sapphires) appear to contain three- or six-pointed stars inside the stone, in an effect known as asterism.

CASSITERITE ►

Cassiterite is the richest tin ore. Tin was one of the first metals used by humankind. It was mixed with copper to make bronze 8,000 years ago, allowing the manufacture of hard tools and weapons. This discovery was so important it gave its name to a new era – the Bronze Age. Most tin comes from cassiterite, which is found in veins in igneous rock, as well as in sediment deposits.

Tin cans are made of aluminium or steel, coated in a layer of tin

RUTILE ►

Rutile is the most important source of titanium. Titanium is three times as strong as steel and twice as light, making it ideal for use in the manufacture of missiles and aircraft. Today, 95 per cent of the world's titanium is used to make titanium dioxide, the main ingredient of white paint (used here for road markings).

RUTILATED QUARTZ

Rutile needles form in quartz

Storage tank for used nuclear fuel rods

Uraninite is known as "pitchblende" when it forms in a massive habit

◄ URANINITE

Uraninite is a radioactive mineral. It is the main ore for uranium and radium. Uranium is used to generate nuclear power. More than 100,000 tonnes (98,420 tons) of uraninite must be mined to produce 25 tonnes of reactive uranium. This is the amount a typical nuclear power station uses every year. Today, much of the uranium used is recycled from dismantled nuclear bombs. Uraninite is mostly found in compact clusters known as pitchblende.

Cobalt used to colour the glass bright blue

SULPHIDES

The minerals in this group are made up of sulphur combined with another mineral, usually a metal. Sulphides include some of the world's most important metal ores, such as cinnabar (mercury ore), galena (lead ore), sphalerite (zinc ore), and chalcopyrite (copper ore). Most sulphides are dense, brittle, and look a little like metal. A few sulphides, such as orpiment and realgar, are clear, light, and shiny. Sulphosalts are compounds of sulphur, in which sulphur bonds directly with a semi-metal such as arsenic, bismuth, or antimony.

◄ LEAD-FRAMED WINDOWS

Lead is a soft, easily worked metal that was widely used in the past for pipes, roofs, and paint pigments. It is now used in electrical batteries, metal alloys, and to shield against X-rays. Lead is easy to shape, so it was used to put together stained-glass windows. H-sectioned bars of lead were bent to fit around the fragments of glass in the window and hold them together.

Lead frames hold the stained glass together

▲ CINNABAR

Usually a bright, brick-red crimson, cinnabar typically crystallizes around hot springs or in volcanic veins. Because it contains so much mercury (up to 85 per cent or more), it is our main source of mercury. Mercury is used in thermometers (shown right) and other scientific instruments. Powdered cinnabar was once widely used as a red paint pigment called vermilion. This pigment is no longer used because, like all mercury compounds, it is poisonous.

Chunk of galena showing cubic and octahedral (eight-sided) crystals

sulphides

Mercury in thermometer

Massive galena forms in volcanic veins

▲ GALENA CUBIC CRYSTALS

Made from sulphur and lead, galena sometimes forms distinctive grey cubic crystals, making it one of the most recognizable minerals. Galena is a natural semiconductor (transmits electricity) and the forerunner of most electronic gadgets we know today. Galena crystals were used in the very first crystal radio sets. The best crystals come from Germany, France, Mexico, and the Tri-State Mining District (Kansas-Missouri-Oklahoma), USA.

GALENA (LEAD ORE) ►

Around three million tonnes of lead ore are mined every year, mostly from large massive habits found in hydrothermal veins. The main producers are Australia, China, and the USA. Once the ore has been brought to the surface, 90 per cent of the material needs to be removed before the metal can be separated by smelting (heating and melting). However, most of the lead we use today is recycled from scrap, which uses far less energy.

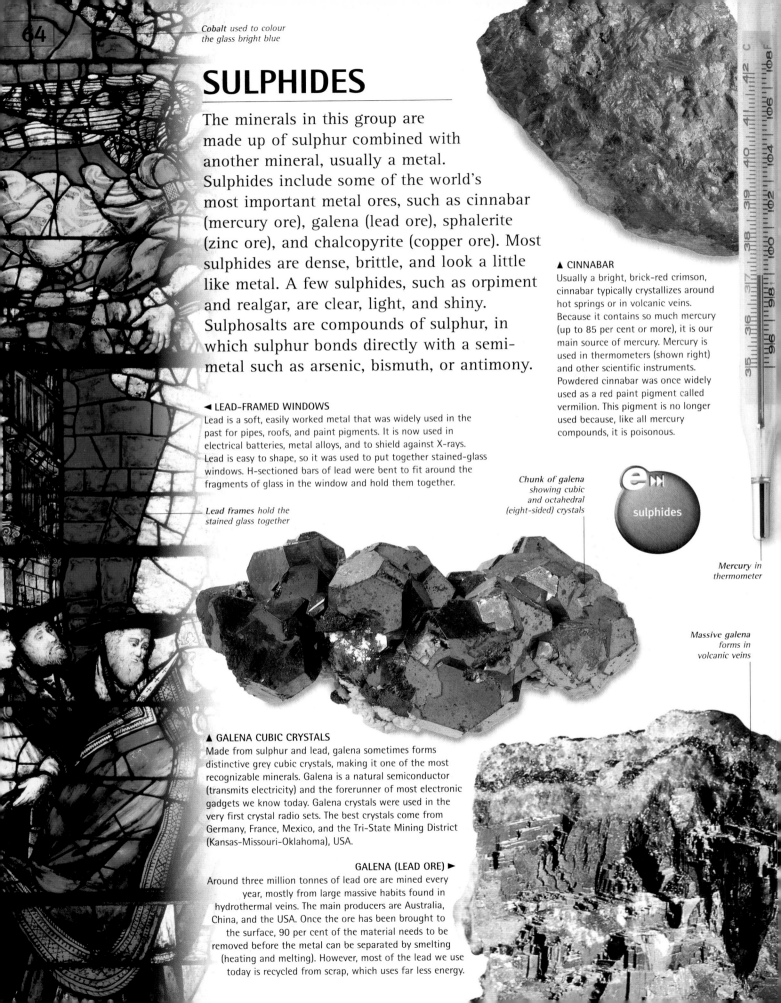

▲ CHALCOCITE

Chalcocite is a mixture of copper and sulphur. Typically 80 per cent copper, its sulphur content is fairly easy to separate off. Unfortunately, chalcocite (also known as chalcosine) is quite rare. The best deposits are virtually mined out. Today, the main copper-producing ore is chalcopyrite, less rich in copper than chalcocite, but more widely found.

▲ ORPIMENT

Lemon-coloured orpiment is one of the Earth's most strikingly coloured minerals. It was once used as a yellow pigment in paint. Highly unstable, orpiment disintegrates over time. The Greek philosopher Theophrastus gave orpiment the name *arsenikon*. The deadly poison it contains – arsenic – got its name from this word. Like all arsenic-rich minerals, it smells of garlic when it is heated.

▲ REALGAR

Bright red realgar is as distinctively coloured as orpiment, just as unstable, and just as deadly. Like orpiment, it is a sulphide of arsenic. The ancient Chinese carved it into ornaments, which have now disintegrated. Realgar's name comes from the arabic, *rahj al ghar*, meaning "powder of the mine".

PRESERVED IN PYRITE

Pyrite replaces organic materials

Living things can be preserved in many ways, but one of the most common is by pyritization. In this chemical process, iron sulphide minerals, called pyrites, gradually form. As buried organic material slowly disintegrates, it is replaced, molecule by molecule, by pyrites. Over millions of years organic remains, like this ammonite, retain their shape but are transformed into pyrites.

TELLURIDES AND ARSENIDES ▶

In tellurides and arsenides, tellurium and arsenic virtually take the place of sulphur in the chemical structure. They are otherwise so similar to sulphides, however, that they are classified with them. Tellurides, in particular sylvanite and calaverite, are among the few minerals that contain gold. The 1890s gold rush to Cripple Creek in Colorado, USA, was based on a find of telluride gold minerals, such as sylvanite.

SYLVANITE

SULPHOSALTS

ENARGITE
This rare mineral is a compound of arsenic, copper, and sulphur. It is rich in copper. Good crystals are found in places like Butte, Montana, USA, Sonora in Mexico, and the Cerro de Pasco in Peru. Enargite often forms very distinctive, star-shaped, twinned crystals known as trillings.

PROUSTITE
Proustite is a compound of silver, antimony, and sulphur. One of the few sulphide minerals that is neither metallic nor opaque, it forms beautiful wine-red crystals that are sometimes cut to make gemstones. This mineral is sometimes called "ruby silver". It is often found in silver mines.

BOURNONITE
A combination of copper, lead, antimony, and sulphur, bournonite forms chunky, prismatic (tablet-shaped) crystals. Sometimes it develops remarkable twinned crystals in the shape of a cog wheel, leading to its English name of "cog wheel ore". Copper, antimony, and lead can all be extracted from it.

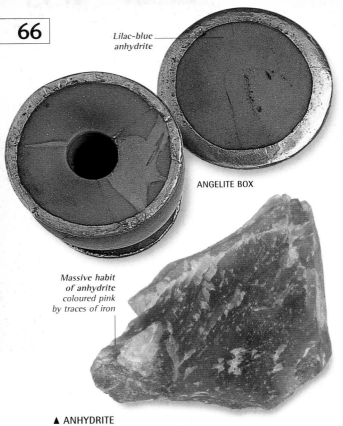

Lilac-blue anhydrite

ANGELITE BOX

Massive habit of anhydrite coloured pink by traces of iron

SULPHATES AND OTHERS

Sulphates are compounds in which one or more metals combine with sulphate (a combination of sulphur and oxygen). Sulphates typically form when sulphates are exposed to air as evaporites or as deposits left by hot volcanic water. All are soft and pale, often with transparent to translucent crystals. There are more than 200 different kinds of sulphate, of which the most common is gypsum. This is a soft, sedimentary rock-forming mineral, with many industrial uses. However, most sulphates are rare and occur only in a few places.

▲ ANHYDRITE

Anhydrite is a translucent, brittle mineral, that ranges in colour from white to brown and forms in thick beds. It is often found mixed in with gypsum, halite, and limestone. In fact, some beds of anhydrite form when the gypsum dries out. When anhydrite dries, it shrinks, so layers of anhydrite are often contorted or riddled with cracks and cavities. Anhydrite crystals are rare, because water usually turns them back to gypsum. Lilac-blue anhydrite is called angelite, because of its "angelic" colour.

FORMS OF GYPSUM

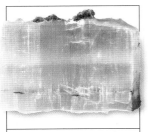

DESERT ROSE
In hot deserts, water often evaporates from shallow, salty basins. Here, gypsum can grow around grains of sand to form flower-like clusters of flat, bladed crystals, called "desert roses". Cockscomb barite forms similar roses, but the gypsum petals are better defined. Namibia in southern Africa is famous for its desert roses.

SATIN SPAR
Although gypsum usually looks dull and powdery, it sometimes forms clear or silky white, threadlike crystals. This form, called satin spar, is treasured for its satin look and is used for carved jewellery and ornaments. Geologists use the word spar to describe any white or light-coloured crystals that are easily broken.

DAISY GYPSUM
When gypsum forms from small pockets of moisture on the surface of rocks, it can often grow in radiating, overlapping patterns of crystals. They are called daisy gypsum because they look like daisies. Sometimes, they even have a tiny yellow spot in the centre to complete the daisy effect.

Porous texture makes it easier to paint

Facial features carve easily because alabaster is soft

◄ GYPSUM (ALABASTER)

Gypsum forms in thick beds where saline (salty) water from shallow seas or salt lakes has evaporated. Gypsum comes in many different varieties, each with its own name (see above). When anhydrite deposits are moistened by surface water, they form fine-grained gypsum. When heated and dried, this is the form that is used as the base for most plasters, including plaster of Paris. Left alone, it is better known as alabaster. This white, ornamental stone has been used in fine carvings since Ancient Egyptian times. This alabaster sculpture comes from the medieval tomb of a knight.

Stained to look like marble

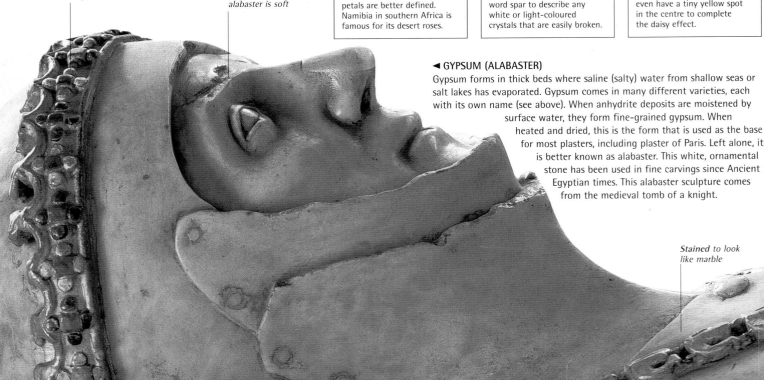

EPSOM
SALTS

TUNGSTEN
FILAMENT

COPPER PANS

EPSOMITE ►
Epsomite is one of only a few sulphate minerals that dissolve in water. As a result, large crystals are rare. It tends to form as a white deposit on limestone cave walls or around hot springs. Its chemical form is hydrated magnesium sulphate, but it is better known as Epsom salts from the mineral waters in Epsom, England, where it was discovered. Epsom salts are used to treat mild indigestion.

WOLFRAMITE ►
Tungstates are closely related to sulphates. Tungsten replaces sulphur and the resulting tungsten-oxygen pairing then combines with another metal. Wolframite and scheelite are the main ores for tungsten, which is used for, amongst other things, making light-bulb filaments. Tungsten's melting point, 3,410°C, 6,170°F, is higher than any other metal.

CHALCANTHITE ►
Bright blue chalcanthite occurs where copper ores are exposed to air. It is the natural form of copper sulphate. Because it dissolves in water, it is usually only found in dry regions. Large deposits were once mined in Chile. This reddish metal is used for making everything from copper pans to electrical wires, because it conducts heat and electricity well.

FORMS OF BARITE

COCKSCOMB
Barite (barium sulphate) is a common mineral. It often forms in hot volcanic waters. Sometimes it grows in thin, blade-like crystals that cluster in a formation that looks like the crest of a cock or a rooster (shown here). When these crested barite cockscombs are stained red with iron, they are known as "barite roses".

CRYSTALLINE
Barite crystals can also form in sheets, fibres, or transparent, colourless, prismatic crystals (shown here), which can be very large. Large masses of barite are exploited for the metal barium. Barium is useful because it is inert (chemically inactive). The main use of barium is as a filler in paints, glass, and toothpaste.

e►► sulphates

Lead ore forms a dark groundmass

CROCOITE

WULFENITE

Splinter-like crystals

Thin, square crystals

◄ CROCOITE
Chromates are a combination of chromium and oxygen. When metallic elements combine with chromates, they produce rare and brightly coloured minerals. Crocoite, a combination of chromate and lead, is a chromium ore. The most famous examples come from Dundas in Tasmania, Australia, where some specimens have slender, prismatic crystals up to 20 cm (8 in) long. Most specimens are made up of small splinter-like crystals or have no crystals at all.

WULFENITE ▲
Molybdates combine molybdenium and oxygen. When metallic elements combine with molybdates, they form dense and brittle compounds. Wulfenite, a combination of molybdate and lead, is easily identified by its striking square-shaped crystals, which resemble interlocking plastic tiles. Usually yellow, they can also be white, red, or orange. The brightest orange crystals came from Chah-Karbose in Iran.

Sea-salt stacks
piled up to dry

HALIDES

Halides are minerals that form when a metal combines with one of the five halogen elements – fluorine, chlorine, bromine, iodine, and astatine. The best known is halite, or rock salt (sodium chloride), from which we make table salt. Like rock salt, many of the halides are soluble (they dissolve easily in water), which is why they often occur only under special conditions. Halite is so common that, despite its solubility, it is found in huge deposits all around the world and has a wide range of industrial uses.

▲ SALT MOUNTAINS
Most halite is mined from thick beds of salt left behind as ancient oceans dried out. It is then left in huge mounds to dry. Some halite forms as water evaporates in salty lakes, such as Utah's Salt Lake. Salt is also used to preserve meat and fish and to make food tasty. Although the human body relies on a regular intake of naturally occurring salts to keep its system balanced, too much salt is unhealthy.

TYPES OF HALITE

ORANGE HALITE
When halite crystallizes, it usually forms cube-shaped crystals. These cubic crystals can often be seen in unrefined sea salt. In nature, however, large halite crystals are rare because the minerals dissolve so easily in water. Where they do occur, they come not only in white but also in colours such as orange and pink.

BLUE HALITE
Some colour changes in halites are produced by bacteria. Some are caused by exposure to natural radiation. Gamma rays turn halite first amber, then deep blue. The blue colour comes from specks of sodium metal. These specks are created when radiation knocks the electrons about within the crystal's structure.

HOPPER CRYSTAL
One of the most striking halite habits is the hopper crystal. The cube-shaped hopper crystals get their name because their sides are indented in a way that resembles the hoppers (containers) on a mine conveyor belt. The indentation occurs because the edges of the crystal face grow faster than the centre.

HARVESTING SEA SALT ▶
Some countries, especially tropical islands, such as the West Indies and Cape Verde, still harvest salt from the sea – the oldest and most labour-intensive method. Sea water is pumped into large, shallow pans and then left to evaporate in the sun. The salt left behind (a tiny proportion) is harvested by hand and sent to a refining plant, where most of it is turned into other chemicals, such as chlorine.

halides

ATACAMITE

Atacamite is a bright-green copper chloride halide. It gets its name from the Atacama Desert in Chile, one of the driest regions in the world, where the best specimens are found. Atacamite forms only in very dry places where copper sulphide minerals are exposed to the air. Typically, it forms in association with malachite, azurite, and quartz, as well as rarer minerals such as chrysocolla, connellite, pseudomalachite, cornetite, and brochantite. Atacamite is very absorbent.

Bright-green malachite, often found with atacamite

Blue John showing bands of coloured crystals

◄ BANDED FLUORITE

Fluorite, another halide, is the only mineral, apart from quartz, that comes in such a variety of colours. In pure form it is colourless, but impurities turn it every shade of the rainbow, from intense purple to bright green. It also glows in the dark under ultraviolet light, giving us the word "fluorescent". Most fluorites are a single colour, but some form in coloured bands. One of the best-known banded fluorites is Blue John, a corruption of its French name, *Bleu Jaune* (Blue Yellow). It is also known as Derbyshire Spar, after the English county in which it is found. It was discovered in the 18th century by miners looking for sources of lead in Derbyshire's caves. It was fashionable to have objects, like this goblet, made of Blue John.

Molten metal helped to flow by flux made from fluorite

FLUORITE ►

Fluorite gets its name from the Latin word meaning "to flow", because it is mainly used as a flux – a substance that lowers the melting point – in steel and aluminium processing. It helps the molten metal flow more easily, and, at the same time, it helps to remove impurities such as sulphur from the metal. Fluorite is a common mineral found in hydrothermal veins and limestones. It is the only source of fluorine, a chemical that is often added to drinking water and toothpaste (as fluoride) to strengthen teeth.

Glass-like, cubic crystals

SYLVITE ►

Sylvite is a chloride chemically very similar to halite. Like halite, it formed in massive beds on ancient seabeds, but unlike halite, it contains potassium (or potash) rather than sodium. Ancient sylvite beds are a major source of potash, which is a main ingredient in fertilizers, used by farmers (see right) all over the world. A quarter of the world's sylvite is mined in Saskatchewan, in Canada. Sylvite crystals do occur (as shown above), but they are quite rare.

CARBONATES AND OTHERS

Carbonate minerals form when a carbonate (carbon and oxygen) combines with metals or semi-metals. Minerals in this group are soft and dissolve easily in acidic substances. Many carbonates form when minerals on Earth's surface are altered by the acidity of the air and rain. Nitrate, borate, and phosphate minerals form when nitrate, borate, or phosphate combine with one or more metallic elements. Phosphates tend to be soft, brittle, and colourful.

▼ CALCITE FORMATIONS

Calcite is made from calcium, carbon, and oxygen. It is one of the Earth's most common rock-forming minerals. Calcite, formed from the tiny shells of dead sea creatures, is the main ingredient in limestone. Mounds of travertine (a form of calcite) form where hot, mineral-rich waters erupt on the Earth's surface in geysers. These mounds at the Fly Geyser in the Black Rock Desert, Nevada, USA, have formed around mining pipes that are no longer used. Calcite stalactites and stalagmites also form in caves.

Travertine calcite is coloured brown by rusty water

◄ ARAGONITE

Aragonite, a white mineral, was first discovered in Aragon, Spain. It is chemically identical to calcite, but its crystals form different shapes, including pointed needles. Aragonite often forms in hot springs or on cave walls where it grows in strange coral-like shapes known as "flos ferri" (flower of iron). Some sea creatures release aragonite naturally. The pearly substance inside oyster shells is made from aragonite.

Flos ferri crystals look like corals

◄ MALACHITE

Malachite is named after the Greek for "mallow", since it has the same colour as a mallow leaf. It is a copper carbonate and usually forms as a tarnish or crust on copper ore. Malachite often has distinctive green bands. It has been carved for ornamental use since ancient times. When copper occurs in other minerals, it can give a blue (azurite or chrysocolla) or red (cuprite) colouring.

Malachite is prized for its rich green colour

◄ RHODOCHROSITE

Rosy pink rhodochrosite often forms inside the bubbles of volcanic mineral veins, containing silver, lead, and copper. The small lumps have a black crust of manganese oxide, while the insides show banding in shades of pink. Rhodochrosite is one of the ores of the metal manganese and is usually found as granular (rough) pieces, rather than crystals.

Pink bands are revealed when rhodochrosite is sliced

CALCITE CRYSTALS

ICELAND SPAR
There are more than 300 different forms of calcite crystal. Pure calcite has been valued for its light-refracting qualities since the 17th century. Iceland spar crystals are used to make optical equipment, such as microscopes. Today, most Iceland spar comes from Mexico.

DOGTOOTH SPAR
Dogtooth spar is named after its resemblance to a dog's pointed teeth. They often form clusters in pools in limestone caves. The pointed shape is called a scalenohedron, because the sides form scalene triangles – triangles in which each side is a different length. Often two crystals form together as twins.

NAILHEAD SPAR
Nailhead spar, or tack-head spar, forms crystals that look like nails. The "nails" are made of two rhombohedra – a long rhombohedron topped with a flat rhombohedron. Nailhead spar often forms in caves and mines. The Jewel Cave in South Dakota's Black Hills, USA, gets its name from the sparkling nailhead crystals on the walls.

◄ PHOSPHATES (WAVELLITE)

Wavellite belongs to the class of minerals known as phosphates, which contain a mix of oxygen and the metal phosphorus. Wavellite forms balls of crystals in limestone, chert rock, and granite. When the balls are broken, they show patterns of spoked discs, such as those shown here.

WAVELLITE

PHOSPHATES (APATITE) ►

Apatite is also a phosphate. It is named after the Greek word for trickery because it comes in many colours and is often mistaken for other minerals such as beryl or peridot. Apatite crystals form in metamorphic rock, but most are too small to see. Large crystals, like the one shown here, are rare. Apatite forms an important part of animal teeth and bones. Its main industrial use is in fertilizers.

APATITE

carbonates

Lignite forms the black in the mask

AZTEC MASK DECORATED WITH TURQUOISE TILES

◄ PHOSPHATES (TURQUOISE)

Turquoise is a phosphate and gets its blue-green colour from the presence of copper. It often forms in deserts – the Ancient Egyptians mined turquoise from the Sinai Desert more than 5,000 years ago. It was imported to Europe through Turkey in the Middle Ages – the word turquoise comes from the French for "Turkish". In Central America, turquoise mining began about 1,000 years ago. The Aztecs used it as raw chunks in jewellery, or made it into tiny mosaic tiles as shown in this mask.

TURQUOISE

NITRATES (NITRATINE) ►

Nitratine (sodium nitrate) belongs to the nitrate family. It resembles calcite but is softer and lighter. Nitrates are rare because they dissolve in water. So they are mainly found in dry regions, such as Chile and California, USA. Nitratine mainly comes from Chile's Atacama Desert. It is used for making fertilizers (magnified above) and explosives.

NITRATINE

BORATES (ULEXITE) ►

Ulexite belongs to the borate group of minerals. Sometimes, ulexite occurs in closely packed threadlike fibres known as "TV rock". The fibres act in the same way that fibre optics (used in telecommunications) do, transmitting light along their lengths by internal reflection. Ulexite is often found with borax, a water-soluble mineral found in everything from food preservatives to fibreglass.

ULEXITE

EARLY USES OF MINERALS

Our earliest ancestors used stone tools to help them hunt and kill animals, slice meat, and build shelters. Around the same time, they discovered the rich colour pigments in minerals and used them to create cave paintings. With the rise of the first civilizations some 9,000 years ago, the variety of uses of rocks and minerals began to expand dramatically. People learned how to build in stone, how to use clay to make pots, how write on clay tablets, and how to use metals to fashion everything from weapons and armour to tools, bowls, and ritual objects.

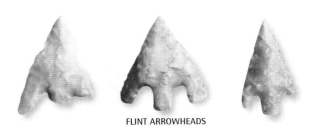

FLINT ARROWHEADS

FLINT SCRAPER

▲ STONE TOOLS
Prehistoric humans were chipping flint to give them sharp edges for knives and handaxes more than two million years ago. Recently, archaeologists found flint knives dating back as far as 2.6 million years at Gona, Ethiopia. Flint provided our ancestors with their first tools, so the period up until the discovery of bronze (*c.* 9000 BC) is known as the Stone Age.

MINERAL PIGMENTS ►
People learned long ago to make coloured pigments by grinding minerals into a paste. Cave paintings dating from 20,000 years ago show the use of four main mineral pigments: red ochre from hematite, yellow ochre from limonite, black from pyrolusite, and white from kaolin (china clay). With the development of the first civilizations, people learned how to use more minerals to create a much wider range of colours – red from realgar, yellow from orpiment, green from malachite, blue from azurite, and ultramarine from lapis lazuli. The rarest pigments, such as lapis lazuli, were highly prized.

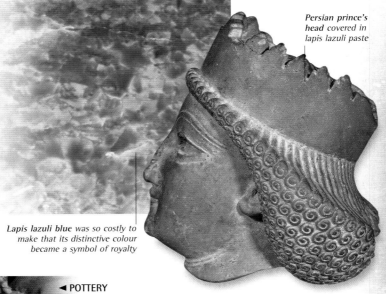

Persian prince's head covered in lapis lazuli paste

"Terracotta Army", made up of 7,000 life-sized figures sculpted from earthenware (the earliest pottery), was buried with China's first emperor

Lapis lazuli blue was so costly to make that its distinctive colour became a symbol of royalty

◄ POTTERY
More than 30,000 years ago, people discovered how to mould soft clay into small statues of humans and animals and to bake them hard in furnaces. No one knows when they learned to shape the clay to make pots, but primitive clay bowls were being made in the Middle East more than 8,000 years ago. Archaeological finds of increasingly sophisticated pottery tell us much about early civilizations. These life-sized earthenware figures of soldiers and horses were buried near the first Chinese Emperor, Qin Shi Huang, in 206 BC. They were intended to guard him in the afterlife.

Sandstone façade protected from erosion by overhanging rock

early uses

ROCKS FOR BUILDING ►
The earliest shelters built by humans were temporary structures, made from sticks and mud. As soon as people began to settle – to farm or to live in towns – they wanted houses that lasted. In the earliest cities, such as Catal Huyuk (modern Turkey), built around 9,000 years ago, people constructed their houses from air-dried mud bricks. The world's oldest stone buildings – the Great Pyramids – were designed as tombs for the Ancient Egyptian pharaohs. Sometimes, buildings were carved into the rock, such as those from the 4th-century BC city of Petra, Jordan (shown here).

◄ **METAL MONEY**
With the first human settlements, trading became part of human life. People needed units of currency (money) with a fixed value. The first currencies were made from shells or beads. These were later replaced by durable, valuable metals, such as gold and silver, which could be easily melted and formed in regular shapes. The earliest coins, dating from the 7th century BC, were found in Lydia (modern Turkey) and were made from electrum (a mix of gold and silver). Doubloons and other Spanish coins were made from gold taken from Central America.

16TH-CENTURY
SPANISH DOUBLOON

Petra Treasury modelled on Greek architectural style

DANGEROUS MINERALS

Some minerals, such as the poison arsenic, have been known to be dangerous since the earliest times. Others, such as lead, have been more stealthy killers. The Romans were probably poisoned by the lead that lined their water pipes. In 16th-century Europe, noble women, including Queen Elizabeth I (shown here), applied a paste made from cerussite (white lead) on their faces to achieve a fashionably pale look. However, cerussite was so caustic that it burnt the face, leaving marks and scars.

Scales used to weigh the salt

▲ **PRECIOUS SALT**
Salt (from halite) has been treated as a precious mineral since ancient times, both for health and as a food preservative. A Chinese book on pharmacy, *Peng-Tzao-Kan-Mu,* written some 4,700 years ago, recommended the consumption of salt for health reasons. Ancient Egyptian art showed salt-making as an important activity. Roman soldiers were paid a regular salt allowance, called a salarium. Even in medieval times, people were being paid a salary – in salt – as this 14th-century painting illustrates. Salt also denoted a person's social status at local banquets, when the less privileged sat "below (beyond) the salt" at the dining table. Throughout history, wars have been fought over access to precious salt reserves.

GEMSTONES

Most minerals are dull or made of small crystals. However, a few are richly coloured and form large, striking crystals. The colour, sparkle, and rarity of these gemstones has made them treasured across cultures and ages. There are more than 3,000 minerals, but only 130 form gemstones. The most valuable of these – diamonds, emeralds, rubies, and sapphires – are known as precious gemstones and are prized for their brilliance (brightness), rarity, and hardness. The more common gemstones, such as beryls, garnets, and peridots, are referred to as semi-precious gemstones.

Light is reflected through the front of the stone

BELLE EPOQUE DIAMOND NECKLACE (1900s)

Colourless, brilliant-cut diamond

◄ DIAMOND MINE
Natural diamonds are incredibly old. Most formed deep in the Earth under extreme heat and pressure up to three billion years ago. Most of these are then brought up to the surface in volcanic pipes filled with kimberlite rock. However, the Argyle mine in Western Australia (shown here) – the world's largest diamond mine – extracts its diamonds from lamproite rock.

83-CARAT UNCUT DIAMOND

DIAMOND JEWELLERY ►
Most diamonds are clear and colourless, but they hide within them a rainbow of colours that can flash dramatically as light hits them at different angles – causing refraction and dispersion of the light. When jewellers cut diamonds to make jewels like those in this necklace, they aim to make the most of this sparkling "fire".

◄ EXAMINING A STONE
Gemstones often look like dull pebbles until they are cut and polished by a skilled lapidarist (gem-cutter). It is very close and detailed work, usually done under a magnifying glass. To cut smooth facets, a rough gemstone is typically glued to a stick and held against a rotating, polishing wheel.

GEMSTONE CUTS

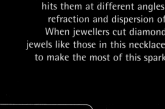

BRILLIANT

ROSE

CABOCHON

PEAR

STEP

Different styles of cutting are used to bring out a stone's best qualities. Opaque or translucent semi-precious gemstones are typically cut into a smooth oval, which is rounded on top and flat underneath. This is called cabochon. Clear precious gemstones, such as diamonds, are usually cut with a series of mirror-like facets (surfaces) to make them sparkle. Coloured stones, such as emeralds and rubies, are step-cut to bring out the rich hues (colours) in the stone. All other cuts are variations of these two. Pear cuts, for example, are pear-shaped with a large flat top.

gemstones

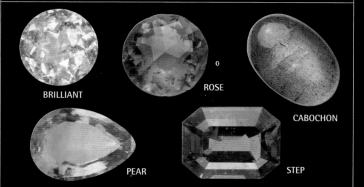

Minute, closely packed silica spheres create a shimmering, opalescent effect

Emerald

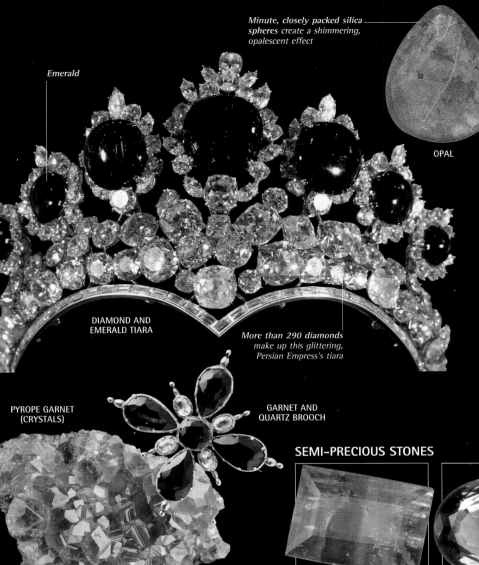

DIAMOND AND EMERALD TIARA

More than 290 diamonds make up this glittering, Persian Empress's tiara

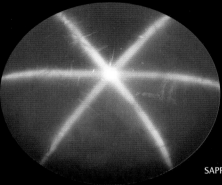

OPAL

◄ GLITTERING JEWELS

Gemstones are not simply colourful. Most sparkle and shine in the light in a variety of ways. The best opals display an extraordinary rainbow play-of-colour called "opalescence", caused by the diffraction (breaking up) of light by minute balls of silica within the stone. Star sapphires show star-shaped lines. This effect, called asterism, is caused by light reflecting off tiny needles of rutile within the gem. Jewellers making a tiara, like the one shown here, use different gemstone cuts, colours, and combinations to bedazzle people when the wearer walks into a brightly lit ballroom or stateroom.

SAPPHIRE

PYROPE GARNET (CRYSTALS)

GARNET AND QUARTZ BROOCH

SEMI-PRECIOUS STONES

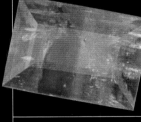

TOURMALINE
Tourmaline has the greatest colour range of any gem. There are even crystals that are pink at one end and green at the other, as shown here. They are called watermelon tourmaline, because the pink and green looks like the flesh and rind of a watermelon. Tourmalines were highly prized by the Russian Tsars.

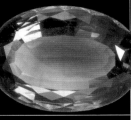

AMETHYST
Amethyst is a gem variety of the common mineral quartz. It comes in colours varying from pale mauve to deep violet. These are caused by iron impurities. The best amethysts come from Brazil, India, and Russia, where they are found in geodes (rock hollows). The biggest amethyst geodes are large enough to crawl inside.

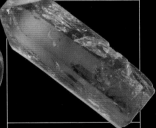

TOPAZ
Topaz comes in a wide variety of colours, from clear to red. Colourless topaz is easily mistaken for diamond. The dark-orange topaz shown here is called hyacinth topaz. Topaz crystals form in igneous rock and can grow to enormous lengths. The biggest-known topaz, found in Brazil, weighs more than 272 kg (600 lb).

▲ GEMS FROM THE DEEP EARTH

The unique combination of extreme pressure and heat deep beneath the ground can create the hard, darkly coloured gems, peridot and garnet. There are many different kinds of garnet – their chemistry is very varied. The pyrope in the brooch here is blood red because it contains some chromium, grossular is orange or pink because of traces of iron and manganese.

◄ ORGANIC GEMSTONES

Organic gemstones are gemstones formed by living things, rather than minerals from the Earth. They include pearl (shown here), amber, and jet. Pearls form inside the shells of shellfish, such as oysters, especially those that live in warm waters. They typically grow in layers, building up around a grain of sand. If a pearl is sawn in two, the layers can be seen under a microscope, like layers of an onion. The longer a pearl takes to form, the larger it will be.

WHITE PEARL

OYSTER SHELL

ARTIFICIAL GEMS ►

Gemstones are valuable because they are rare or hard to get out of the rock. As a result, people have tried to create them artificially. Most gems can now be made synthetically by melting the right chemicals and allowing them to crystallize under the right conditions. Many are very hard to tell from the real thing. Cubic zirconia "diamonds" are made from zirconium oxide crystals that are almost as hard and sparkly as real diamonds.

CUBIC ZIRCONIA

DECORATION

Besides gemstones, many other rocks and minerals are used for decoration. Although never clear or sparkling like gems, they often have vivid colours and patterns. Ornamental stone is quarried to decorate the façades (fronts) of buildings. Almost any rock can be ornamental, as long as it polishes well and resists weathering. Typical examples of ornamental stone include marble, limestone, travertine, slate, and granite. Colourful non-precious minerals, used for carving ornaments, statues, and more functional objects, include agate, onyx, jade, and jasper.

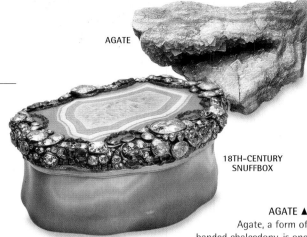

AGATE

18TH-CENTURY SNUFFBOX

AGATE ▲
Agate, a form of banded chalcedony, is one of the most popular minerals for ornamental work. In the 16th century, a large agate ornament industry grew up around the Idar-Oberstein district of Germany. Ring agate, with its circular bands, is particularly effective in ornaments like this 18th-century snuffbox. Today, much of the agate used in ornamental work has been artificially stained.

▼ ONYX
Onyx is a variety of agate with black-and-white alternating bands. Carnelian onyx has white-and-red bands. Sardonyx (shown below) has brown-and-white bands. Onyx has been popular for carving since Roman times. Indeed, the Romans called any beautiful stone for carving, onyx. This carved snuff bottle was made in China in the 19th century.

SARDONYX

JASPER ►
Jasper is a mottled brick-red stone related to quartz. It is actually a kind of chert (sedimentary) rock, which forms hard nodules in limestone. Red jasper (shown below) gets its colour from traces of iron, while green jasper gets its colour from tiny fibres of the mineral actinolite. It is quite dull when found but polishes well. Jasper pebbles glisten attractively when wet.

18TH-CENTURY VASE

JASPER

JADE ►
Jade is the ornamental variety of not one but two minerals – nephrite and jadeite. Both these minerals can be white, colourless, or red, but the most sought-after kind is pale emerald green. Jade is particularly cherished in China, where it has been carved into jewellery, ornaments, and small statues for thousands of years. One of China's best-known archaeological finds was the tomb of the Han prince Liu Sheng and princess Tou Wan, dating from 113 BC. Each body is completely encased in a suit of armour made from more than 2,000 small plates of jade, sewn together with gold wire. The Chinese believed that jade would protect their bodies from decay – and perhaps evil spirits, too – and give them immortality.

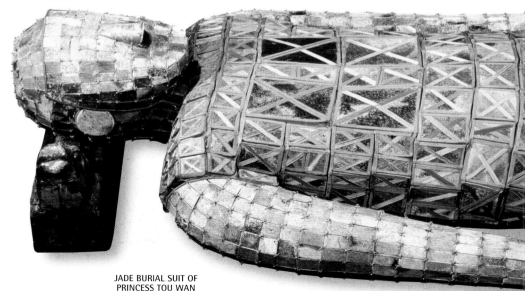

JADE BURIAL SUIT OF PRINCESS TOU WAN

◄ WATERPROOF DECORATION
Much stone is not only tough and colourful, but also waterproof and a good conductor of heat. This makes it the perfect material for ornamental washrooms and courtyards in warm climates. Water from fountains and baths can flow over the stone without doing any damage. The stones conduct heat well and quickly drain away heat, so they feel cool to the touch.

SCULPTING THE ROCK ►
Techniques for carving stone have changed little in thousands of years. The main tools are still a steel chisel and a hammer. Some sculptors use a pneumatic (air-powered) mallet. However, the basic technique is the same – to bang the chisel over the stone, chipping away small pieces of rock at a time.

WHITE MARBLE ►
White marble has been a favourite material for sculpting since the time of Ancient Greece. This striking marble statue of a horse from the Acropolis in Athens dates from about 490 BC. Like all the best white marble, it has a creamy glow because it is not completely opaque – light penetrates about an inch below the surface to crystals that reflect light.

◄ ROCK SURFACES
Granite's strength and durability make it an important building stone, but its rich colours and the attractive mottle of its large grains make it a popular ornamental stone, too, particularly when it is cut flat and polished. It is often used to cover exterior walls. It is a low-maintenance stone, resistant to spills and heat, so it makes an ideal material for floors and kitchen countertops.

decoration

Plates of jade

Silky smooth surface from carved marble

Handle of bone lashed together with sealskin

Butchering knife made from hand-beaten copper

METALS IN HISTORY

Ancient civilizations first used metal about 6,000 years ago, when they hammered native gold and silver into ornaments. Different cultures soon discovered that rocks held many other metals, including copper, tin, iron, and lead. Each had its own unique characteristics. What made metals special were their durability and malleability – they could be shaped into anything from simple weapons and tools to huge machines, and they lasted. These qualities have helped metal to play a key part in the progress of human technology.

▲ BEATEN COPPER
Copper was one of the first metals to be used for making everyday objects, because it is easily extracted from the ground. Like gold, it can be beaten into shape, like this ornate Inuit blade. Evidence from around Lake Superior, USA, shows that ancient peoples, known as the "Old Copper Culture", began mining copper about 6,000 years ago. Copper remained the main metal used by Native Americans for thousands of years.

LATE BRONZE-AGE ARMOUR

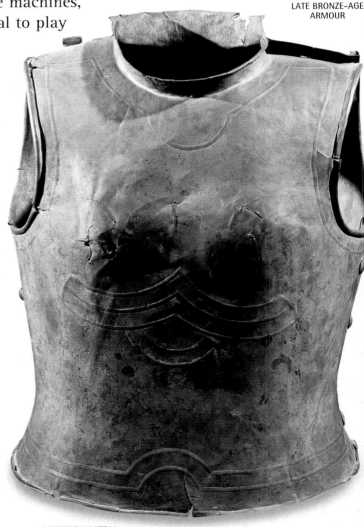

▲ THE DISCOVERY OF BRONZE
Learning to mix copper with arsenic – and later with tin – to make bronze, was a breakthrough in metalworking. The Bronze Age lasted from around 3000 BC, when bronze was discovered in Southwest Asia, until around 1000 BC, when iron was first widely used. The bronze frieze shown here, which dates from c. 840 BC, covered the huge, wooden gates that led into the Assyrian city of Balawat in modern-day Iraq.

◄ COPPER SMELTING
The first metals used by humankind were native metals. Native metals are rare, so it was a great leap forward when metalworkers first discovered how to obtain metals from ores (rocks containing minerals) about 5,000 years ago. They heated the ore until the metals inside melted and ran out in a liquid form. This process, known as smelting, is shown in this woodcut. The workman loading the ore into the furnace wears a safety mask as protection against the fumes. Copper was the first metal to be smelted, from copper-rich sulphide minerals, such as chalcopyrite.

▲ MILITARY METAL
Copper is too soft to make a blade that stays sharp. Early cultures found that adding tin to copper made it much tougher. This alloy is known as bronze. The first swords and suits of armour were bronze. When the Ancient Greeks famously attacked the city of Troy in Asia Minor, they may have wanted to win control of the city's famous bronze trade. Bronze was brought to the rest of Europe – where this chest armour was made – by roving Greek merchants.

◄ IRON PILLAR, NEW DELHI

The problem with making bronze is that tin is rare and costly. About 4,500 years ago, people – perhaps the Hittites in Anatolia (modern Turkey) – learned how to smelt iron. Iron ore was relatively common and cheap. Ironworking started in India about 3,500 years ago. This 7-m-high (23-ft) iron pillar in New Delhi, India, was erected during the Gupta dynasty in the 5th century AD. The quality of the iron used for making the pillar is very pure and it has not rusted at all, despite the warm, moist climate.

Sanskrit inscription shows that the pillar was raised in memory of King Chandragupta

ALCHEMY

Early knowledge of chemistry, including the properties of metals and acids, came from the work of alchemists. These early "scientists" were interested in finding the secret of turning base metals, such as lead, into precious metals, such as silver or gold. Some alchemists even tried to find the secret of immortality through their experiments. Alchemists were especially interested in mercury, which could be combined with other metals to make coloured powders. The study of alchemy began in Ancient Egypt and had spread across Asia and into Europe by the Middle Ages.

metals in history

THE AGE OF IRON AND STEEL ►

Iron can be turned into a tougher metal, called steel, by heating it and alloying (mixing) it with carbon. Indian metalworkers discovered this process more than 2,000 years ago. However, it was only at the end of the 18th century that a process for mass-producing iron and steel was developed in England, leading to the Industrial Revolution. England's first ironworks factory (shown here) was built at Coalbrookdale. Out of this came the whirring, clanking, smoking machines of the modern age – from steam locomotives to weaving machines.

Chimneys spewed out noxious pollution

Cast iron allowed engineers to create larger, stronger structures

Ironworks were usually situated close to supplies of coal and iron ore

◄ IRON IN CONSTRUCTION

Early iron was usually wrought (hammered) into shape by hand. The process of casting – pouring liquid metal into shaped moulds – dates back to the 6th century BC in China. But the increased demand for iron during the Industrial Revolution led to the development of large-scale casting techniques. Although early cast iron was more brittle than wrought iron, it was used for mass-produced machine parts. Engineers also found that cast iron was so strong, it could be used to build bridges, buildings, and other weight-bearing structures. This 18th-century arched bridge at Coalbrookdale, England, was the world's first iron bridge.

Passenger pods made from steel and glass

Steel alloy wheel

Light tubular steel

MODERN METALS

Metals are as much a part of the modern world as they were in the Bronze or Iron Ages. Indeed, metals play a part in almost every aspect of our lives. The cars, trains, aeroplanes, and ships that carry us around are all made of steel. Copper wires carry electrical signals, which power everything from PCs to streetlights. Many of these metals are the same ones that have been known and used for thousands of years – iron, steel, copper, tin, and lead. However, a few crucial new metals have been discovered more recently, such as aluminium and titanium. A whole host of new alloys have been developed to meet the needs of modern technology.

◄ STEEL ALLOYS

Steel is iron hardened and toughened by adding traces of carbon and other substances. The most widely used steel is carbon steel, which has less than 1 per cent carbon. Mild steel for car bodies can have as little as 0.25 per cent carbon. Other steel alloys are made by adding traces of other metals, such as tungsten, to give it special qualities. Manganese and tungsten are used for strength, molybdenum for heat resistance, and nickel and chromium for corrosion (rust) resistance. The steel alloy used to make the UK's giant London Eye wheel, contains titanium for strength and chromium for anticorrosion.

▲ STEEL PRODUCTION

Steel is made in giant steel mills from scrap steel or purified pig iron that is melted in a furnace and poured into moulds to make slabs of steel. These slabs are then reheated and rolled into long, thin strips (shown here). Pig iron is the cooled, molten iron taken directly from a blast furnace. However, it contains 4–5 per cent carbon along with other impurities and is so hard and brittle that it is almost useless. To create steel, most of these impurities must be removed. Many modern steel plants use the basic oxygen process (BOP). This involves blowing a jet of oxygen over the molten iron to oxidize the excess carbon, turning it into carbon dioxide gas.

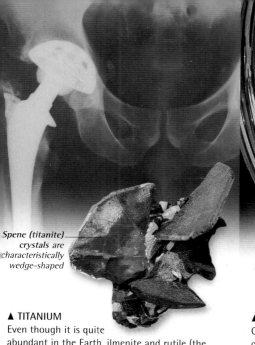

Spene (titanite) crystals are characteristically wedge-shaped

▲ TITANIUM

Even though it is quite abundant in the Earth, ilmenite and rutile (the main titanium ores) were only discovered in the 1790s. Now titanium is one of the most important metals for modern technologies. It resists corrosion, is stronger than steel and almost as light as aluminium. It is used in everything from aircraft alloys to artificial hip replacements (shown above).

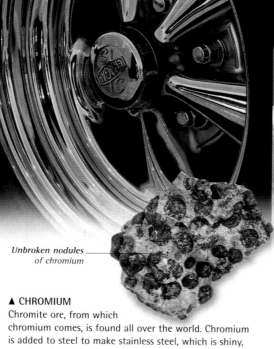

Unbroken nodules of chromium

▲ CHROMIUM

Chromite ore, from which chromium comes, is found all over the world. Chromium is added to steel to make stainless steel, which is shiny, tough, and very resistant to corrosion. The chromium content varies from 10 to 26 per cent. Chromium is also used to plate everyday metal objects, such as bathroom taps, car hubcaps (shown above), and espresso coffee machines, to give them a lasting, shiny look.

Sphalerite crystals range in colour from black to white

▲ ZINC

Sphalerite and smithsonite are the main zinc ores. Zinc has been used since Roman times, when it was combined with copper to make brass. Today, zinc is mainly used for galvanizing steel – a thin coating stops the steel from rusting. A zinc compound is also used as a sunscreen (shown above), reflecting harmful rays away from the skin.

◄ ALUMINIUM

Aluminium is the most abundant of all the Earth's metals and one of the most widely used. Its high electrical conductivity, low weight, and resistance to corrosion means it is valued for everything from overhead power cables (shown here) to food packaging. However, bauxite (its ore) was not discovered until 1808, and a way of extracting aluminium from its ore was not found until 1854. Bauxite is not solid rock like some ores, but a kind of laterite – a loose, weathered material found in the tropics.

modern metals

PROBLEMS OF MINING

Modern mining methods have left vast areas marked by huge craters and have poisoned lakes and vast stretches of streams. Here, a stream polluted with waste-water runoff from a local coal mine flows into the Ohio River, USA. Iron pyrites from the mine causes the reddish-brown colour. In the USA alone, the metal-mining industry released 15,000 tonnes (14,760 tons) of toxic waste into the environment in 2000.

Titanium-rich alloy wings are tough and light

▲ MODERN ALLOYS

The demands for tougher, lighter metals by the aerospace industry has led to the development of numerous new alloys. Many involve titanium or aluminium. A fighter plane, like the F-16XL shown here, may be up to 10 per cent titanium by weight and include a dozen or more different specialized alloys, each performing a different task. For the new A380 Super-Airbus alone, three brand-new aluminium alloys were created, using the metals cobalt, hafnium, molybdenum, and titanium, to give added strength and flexibility, while protecting against stress and corrosion.

MINERALS IN INDUSTRY

Many minerals are used in industry. Some minerals, such as quartz, silica, and gypsum, are extracted in bulk (vast quantities) from sedimentary rocks, such as limestone, clay, and shale. Many of these are important for building, providing materials for making cement and aggregate (pieces of crushed stone or gravel), which, along with cement, make concrete. Others help to purify metals or prepare coal for power stations. Bulk minerals are also used in glass, paint, ceramics, electronics, drugs, and many other products.

GYPSUM

▲ GYPSUM PLASTER
Most modern plaster is made by grinding gypsum to a powder, heating it to dry it, and then adding water. Gypsum plaster was used by the Ancient Egyptians to plaster the Great Pyramid of Giza. Until recently, many buildings in Europe and North America used traditional lime plaster (made from heated limestone), which gives a softer, smoother, whiter finish – but takes a long time to dry. Lime plaster was also used as a surface for frescoes and for making ornamental mouldings. Nowadays, most builders use gypsum plaster (shown above) because it dries quickly to a tough finish.

◄ CALCITE (CHALK)
Most limestone is mainly made up of calcite (calcium carbonate). Chalk is almost pure calcite. Calcite is an incredibly useful mineral, known since ancient times. It is a key ingredient in cement and fertilizer. Pure, finely ground calcite is called "whiting" and is widely used as a filler or pigment in ceramics, paints, paper, cosmetics, plastics, linoleum, and putty.

CALCITE

◄ CEMENT
Cement is the "glue" that holds bricks together in buildings. The Ancient Romans used it to make the world's first concrete dome for the roof of the Pantheon in Rome, Italy, in AD 126. To make the cement, they mixed wet lime with volcanic ash, taken from near the city of Pozzuoli. Today, cement is made from a mixture of limestone (calcite), silica, alumina, gypsum, and iron oxide. Cement also helps to combine aggregates, such as sand and gravel, into concrete.

Pantheon's dome is made from concrete – a mix of cement, sand, and gravel

industrial minerals

▲ NEUTRALIZING ACID LAKES WITH LIME
When limestone is heated in limekilns, it turns to lime, known as quicklime. When quicklime is mixed with water, it becomes hot and swells, making it look "quick", an old-fashioned word for alive. After water is added, it is known as slaked lime and will not react to the water because its thirst has been slaked (satisfied). Lime is widely used as a fertilizer and in water and sewage treatment to reduce acidity. Recently, lime has been used to try to counteract some of the effects of acid rain. Huge quantities of quicklime are sprayed into acid-affected lakes in an effort to neutralize the acidity that kills off life in the lake. This has only been successful in small lakes.

◄ KAOLIN

Kaolin, or China clay, is a soft, white clay named after a hill in China, where it was mined for centuries. It provides the basic material in porcelain and the whiteness in paper. It is made mainly of the mineral kaolinite, but contains traces of other minerals such as feldspar. Deposits form mainly from the weathering of feldspar-rich rocks. In South America, parrots lick kaolin clay to counteract toxins in some of the tropical plant fruit and seeds they eat.

PORCELAIN VASE

Glass is made from silica

Molten glass flows like treacle and can be easily shaped and blown into shapes

CONCRETE ►

Concrete is the cheapest, toughest, and most versatile of all building materials. Almost every major construction project uses concrete. It is made from chunks of hard material called aggregate, bound together by cement. The character of the concrete depends partly on the cement mix, but mainly on the kind of aggregate used. Common aggregates include sand, crushed or broken stone, gravel, boiler ash, and burned clay.

Concrete used to create a runoff ditch as a flood-control measure

COMMONLY USED INDUSTRIAL MINERALS

TALC
Talc is the Earth's softest mineral. It often occurs in a soft rock called soapstone. Soapstone has a long history of being carved and made into ornaments. Powdered soapstone (talcum powder) is used on its own as a drying agent, but it is also used to help make cosmetics, paint, lubricants, and ceramics.

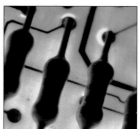

MICA
Mica is a very important mineral, occurring in almost every kind of rock. The most commonly used forms are muscovite and phlogopite – they easily cleave into thin sheets, and resist heat and electricity. This makes mica an ideal choice for insulating electrical components, such as this circuit board.

BORAX
Borax is a soft, light chemical made from minerals, such as colemanite and kernite. Much of it comes from crusts formed in evaporite deposits around lakes in California, USA. Borax has a wide range of industrial uses, including ceramics, glassware, and metalware (shown here). It is used to fuse metal seams.

▲ SILICA

Silica is the name for a group of minerals made of silicon oxide – a combination of the two most abundant elements in the Earth's crust (silicon and oxygen). Silica occurs in a variety of forms, the most common of which is quartz. Quartz is so common that it is found in nearly all mined and quarried materials and is one of the key ingredients in many modern technologies. It is used for glassmaking (shown here), paints, plastics, glues, ceramics, foundry casting, aggregates, oil drilling, farming, and electronics.

MINERALS IN THE HOME

A modern home is built almost entirely out of materials taken from minerals. The only exception is timber, which is used for providing roofs, floors, and structual supports. The foundations that support the house are made of concrete (gravel, sand, and cement). The walls are made of bricks (clay) bound with mortar (limestone). Rooftiles (clay) and plastic guttering (oil) divert the water outside. Inside, water is pumped around the house in metal pipes (copper) for heating and washing. Ceramic (clay) or metal (stainless steel) basins, baths, and heaters hold the water. Windows made from glass (silica) provide natural light, while electrical wiring (copper) provides artificial light, as well as telecommunications and power.

MINERALS USED IN THE HOUSE ▶
Every modern house is made from processed bulk industrial minerals, such as gypsum and limestone, and metals, such as copper and steel. Natural rock, such as granite and marble, is often used decoratively in kitchens and bathrooms. While in the past houses were built from identifiable, local materials, it is almost impossible to trace the origins of the minerals used in a modern house. Just the handbasin may contain borates from California, K-feldspar from Russia, and kaolinite from the Czech Republic.

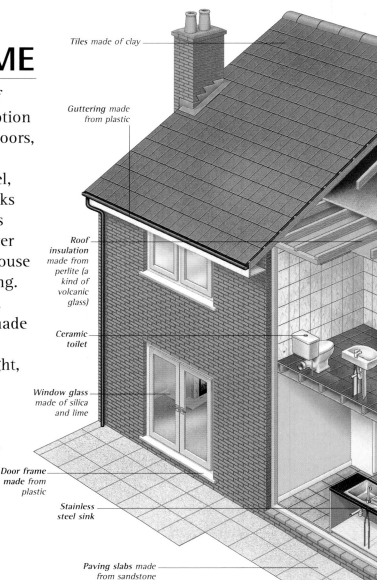

Tiles made of clay

Guttering made from plastic

Roof insulation made from perlite (a kind of volcanic glass)

Ceramic toilet

Window glass made of silica and lime

Door frame made from plastic

Stainless steel sink

Paving slabs made from sandstone

▲ MORTAR (CEMENT, SAND)
Mortar – a mixture of cement, sand, and water – is used in building to bind bricks or stone together. The cement used is usually Portland cement, invented in 1824. It is a mixture of fine lime (calcium hydroxide from heated limestone) with clay or shale.

▲ TILES (CLAY)
In the past, many roofs were covered in slate. Nowadays, most roofs are covered in moulded clay tiles. Traditionally, clay tiles were made by hand and retained their natural colour variation. Modern tiles are machine-made, all coloured the same, and fired in high-temperature kilns.

▲ PIPES (COPPER)
Pipes providing hot water for the bathroom and central heating are usually made from copper because it is cheap and easy to shape. But copper is not so good for drinking-water pipes, because too much copper is toxic for babies.

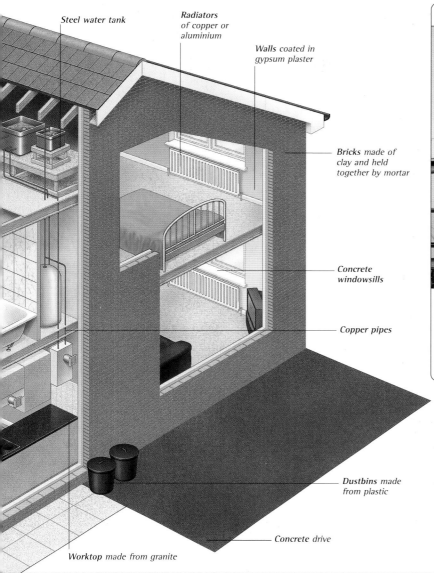

Steel water tank

Radiators of copper or aluminium

Walls coated in gypsum plaster

Bricks made of clay and held together by mortar

Concrete windowsills

Copper pipes

Dustbins made from plastic

Concrete drive

Worktop made from granite

ENVIRONMENTAL BUILDING

Most houses are still built from bricks. In recent years, a range of alternative building materials has been tried. This environmentally friendly house is partly made of straw bales, which insulate it so well it needs very little heating. The upper floors are covered with quilted sheets of fibreglass cloth to block out noise. The house is raised up on cement-filled sandbags. The wattle and metal fence, a mixture of natural and recycled materials, provides privacy. The house is partly solar-powered.

BRICKS ►
The first bricks were made from mud taken from the riverbank. The mud was moulded into blocks and dried in the sun. The idea of heating clay in a kiln to make harder bricks was first thought of 3,500 years ago. Today, the basic process is the same, but a wider range of clays is used, including river clays, shales, and fire clays mined from the ground.

▲ GLASS (SILICA)
The sheet glass in windows is made from silica, soda ash, lime, and a tiny amount of magnesia (magnesium oxide). Other materials, such as selenium or cobalt oxide, are added to remove the green tinge caused by traces of iron. This helps to give a clear view.

▲ PAINT (TITANIUM DIOXIDE)
In the past, people mixed their own housepaints. But for the last century or more, most houses have been decorated in ready-mixed paints, made with linseed oil, turpentine, coloured pigments, and a base. The base used to be lead, but, because lead is poisonous, the base is now titanium dioxide.

▲ FITTED KITCHEN (GRANITE, CLAY)
The best-quality kitchens tend to have work surfaces made from granite. Granite is valued for its durability, heat resistance, and looks. Glazed ceramic tiles (clay) protect the walls from water and grease. Stainless steel (iron) is used for making cookers and sinks.

Black humus made from rotting plants and organic matter

Topsoil rich in humus (rotting plants) and minerals

Subsoil is poor in humus

MINERALS FOR LIFE

Every plant and animal on the Earth depends on minerals for their nutrients – substances essential for life and for growth. Plants get their main nutrients from phosphorus, calcium, and potassium. These are supplemented by much smaller quantities of iron, cobalt, zinc, boron, nickel, manganese, and copper. The plants absorb these minerals from the soil through their roots. Animals, including humans, rely mainly on minerals such as iron, calcium, sodium, and potassium. They get most of these from the food that they eat.

▲ HOW PLANTS GET MINERALS
Plants have a vast surface area of branching roots, which they use to absorb mineral-rich water from the soil. Each root is covered with microscopic root hairs, which draw in the water and send a continuous supply up the stem to the leaves where it is needed.

▲ MINERALS IN SOIL
Soils are a mix of organic matter with minerals, such as silica and iron oxides. Most soils contain all the minerals a plant needs. However, these minerals are not always available in the right amounts. This is why some soils are more fertile than others. As a soil matures, it develops distinct layers with different mineral contents. In areas of heavy rain, minerals are often leached (washed down) through the soil to a deeper layer.

▲ HERBIVORES
Herbivores, such as hippopotamuses and cows, rely entirely on plants for the minerals that they need. Amazingly, plants provide almost all these minerals, though herbivores can sometimes lack calcium and phosphorus. Herbivores often lick salt deposits to make up for a lack of salt (sodium and chloride).

▲ CARNIVORES
Carnivores, such as lions and bears, rely on meat for their minerals. Meat is rich in most of the minerals the animals need to stay healthy, including calcium, chromium, copper, iron, selenium, sulphur, and zinc. However, meat is short of other vital minerals, such as salt, potassium, iodine, and manganese. Carnivores usually supplement their diet with plant foods containing these, in order to stay healthy.

◄ MINERALS IN FOOD
Scientists have identified 16 minerals that people need to have in their diet to stay healthy. Large amounts of the basic nutrient minerals – calcium, sodium, chloride, magnesium, phosphorus, and potassium – are needed. Small amounts of iron and zinc are also needed. Certain minerals, such as selenium, magnesium, and iodine, are only needed in miniscule amounts. Different foods contain different amounts of minerals. However, the same food can contain varying amounts of minerals depending on the type of soil it grew in. The picture here shows which foods supply which basic minerals and vitamins.

Olive oil contains sodium

Pepper has vitamin C, which improves calcium absorption

Milk contains calcium

Nuts contain manganese, phosphorus, and copper

Fresh fruit and vegetables contain phosphorus, sulphur, and potassium

Pulses contain magnesium, potassium, and manganese

Dark-green leafy vegetables contain iron, calcium, and molybdenum

Carrots contain beta carotene, which is converted into vitamin A

Fish contains phosphorus, chromium, iodine, and selenium

Chillis contain vitamin C

minerals for life

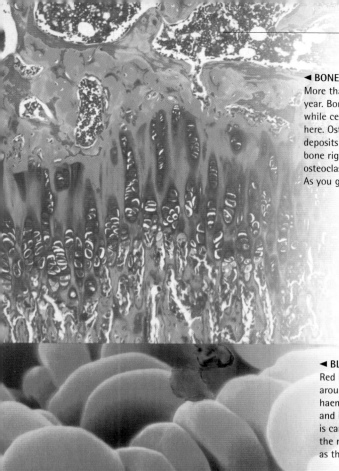

Mineral deposits from osteoblast cells

Milk is one of the best sources of calcium

◄ BONE FORMATION

More than a tenth of your skeleton is replaced each year. Bone cells called osteoclasts clear away dead bone, while cells called osteoblasts create new ones, as shown here. Osteoblasts create rubbery collagen and lay down deposits of calcium and phosphorus, which give the bone rigidity. In young children, osteoblasts outnumber osteoclasts, and more bone is created than destroyed. As you grow older, the balance reverses.

CALCIUM FOR GROWTH ►

Calcium and phosphorus are crucial in the growth of children's bones and teeth. This is why children are encouraged to drink milk and eat cheese and dark green, leafy vegetables. These foods are all rich in calcium. Phosphorus is found in most plant and animal protein.

◄ BLOOD AND IRON

Red blood cells (shown here, greatly magnified) are the cells that carry oxygen around the body. The oxygen is carried inside each cell by a unique molecule called haemoglobin, which contains iron. In the lungs, oxygen attaches itself to the iron and is deliverd to all the tissues by the blood. Haemoglobin glows bright red when it is carrying oxygen, giving oxygen-rich blood its colour. If there is a shortage of iron, the red blood cells cannot carry as much iron and symptoms of breathlessness occur, as the heart pumps faster and the lungs try to make up for the lack of oxygen.

Spinach leaf provides essential iron

◄ SOURCES OF IRON

Iron is essential for all body cells. Although iron is found in a variety of foods, its absorption by the body differs significantly depending on the food. Iron in meat and fish is absorbed much more easily than the iron in fruit, beans, grains, and dark green vegetables such as spinach. Absorption of the iron in these foods can be increased by combining them with sources of vitamin C.

MINERALS FOR HEALTH

People have bathed in mineral-rich waters and natural hot springs to improve their health since the earliest times. The earliest known spa, in Merano, Italy, dates back 5,000 years. At its height in the 18th century, spa-bathing was an upper-class social phenomenon. However, there is some evidence that spa-bathing may have real benefits for diseases like cirrhosis, lead-induced gout, rheumatoid arthritis, and high blood-pressure. Bathing in mineral-rich waters can also be good for the skin – and can be very relaxing. Today, sales of mineral water for drinking are at an all time high.

MINERAL SUPPLEMENTS ►

Lack of iron in the diet over a long period can lead to iron-deficiency anaemia, which makes people look tired and pale. Most people who eat a balanced diet, including red meat such as beef, will not suffer from this. However, vegetarians are more at risk. People often take tablets containing iron to correct iron deficiency, but most doctors believe it is better to eat the right food.

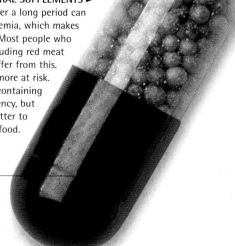

Iron granules housed in edible case

GEOLOGY IN THE FIELD

Geologists collect mineral specimens directly from the landscape, then identify and analyse them using scientific tests. Geologists and other Earth scientists do not just test their theories in laboratories or with mathematical calculations. Instead, they collect their data and test their specimens in the real world – facing bitter winds on mountain tops or braving erupting volcanoes close up. The word used to describe this hands-on outdoor work is fieldwork. For the geologist, the field can mean anything from an Arctic glacier to a deep underwater ocean trench – in fact, anywhere on Earth.

◀ RADIOMETRIC DATA

A geologist uses a Geiger counter or radiometer to measure the amount of radioactivity produced by rock formations. Natural (background) levels of radioactivity result from the decay of the element uranium, which is present in almost all rocks and soils. When uranium decays, it produces the radioactive gas radon, which comes out of the ground continuously. The reading from the Geiger counter can be used to identify the rocks in a particular area, because each rock type has a different radiometric reading.

▲ MEASURING WITH SATELLITES

Tectonic plates can move a lot over millions of years. During a lifetime these movements are very small. Until recently, geologists could not measure such tiny movements. But since the invention of laser measuring systems using satellites, geologists can detect the widening of an ocean by even a few millimetres. Now with the addition of the global positioning system (GPS), geologists can measure how far land moves in a short time. GPS measurements showed that this spot in California, USA (shown above), moved upwards by 38 cm (15 in) and northeast by 21 cm (8 in) in the 1994 Northridge earthquake.

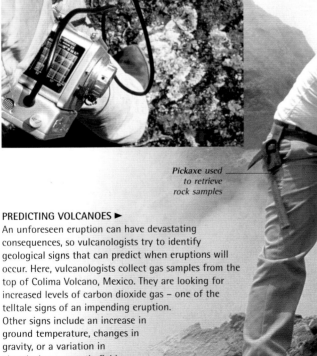

Gas mask protects from poisonous fumes

Pickaxe used to retrieve rock samples

PREDICTING VOLCANOES ▶

An unforeseen eruption can have devastating consequences, so vulcanologists try to identify geological signs that can predict when eruptions will occur. Here, vulcanologists collect gas samples from the top of Colima Volcano, Mexico. They are looking for increased levels of carbon dioxide gas – one of the telltale signs of an impending eruption. Other signs include an increase in ground temperature, changes in gravity, or a variation in electrical or magnetic fields. However, vulcanologists still cannot predict eruptions accurately.

Scuba-diving geologist examining stromatolites

geology

Fossilized mats of bacteria

◄ UNDERWATER GEOLOGY

Geologists sometimes venture to dangerous or difficult places, including the bottom of the ocean. The geologist here is scuba diving in the Caribbean, looking at living stromatolites. Stromatolites, which look like giant stone mushrooms, are ancient communities of bacteria that live in shallow, tropical waters on limestone rock. Each community contains so many bacteria that they build up thick mats of organic matter over the rock. Fossilized stromatolites found in Western Australia date back over 3.5 billion years, providing the earliest evidence of life on Earth.

◄ UNDERSTANDING EARTH'S MAGNETIC FIELD

Rock samples are often brought back to the laboratory for testing. This basalt sample is being loaded into a cryogenic magnetometer to measure the strength and alignment of its magnetic field. The basalt contains grains of iron oxide that indicate the direction of the Earth's magnetic poles when the lava hardened. Geologists use this data to understand changes in Earth's magnetic field over millions of years.

IDENTIFYING SAMPLES ►

High-powered microscopes can help to identify minerals by revealing their crystal structures. They are also used to prepare samples of minerals and fossils (shown here) for further study. Minerals that cannot be identified under a microscope can sometimes be identified by X-ray crystallography. This involves beaming X-rays through a sample. Every crystal has its own unique chemical structure, which diffracts (breaks up) the rays differently.

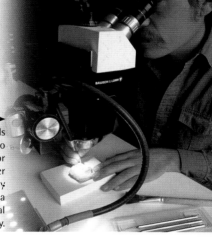

ESSENTIAL FIELD EQUIPMENT ►

You can collect your own rock and mineral samples, when you stroll along the beach or take a walk in the countryside. To get the best out of a rock-hunting expedition, it helps to take some basic equipment with you. You will need a hammer and chisel for extracting rock samples, and goggles and gloves to protect your eyes and hands. Specimens, especially delicate crystals, should be wrapped in newspaper or other protective material, to prevent chipping and scratching, and packed in a secure container.

HAMMER

NEWSPAPER

BUBBLE WRAP

SEALABLE BAG

WIDE CHISEL

PENKNIFE

POINTED CHISEL

PLASTIC BOTTLES

MUSLIN BAG

PROPERTIES

Rocks and minerals can be organized and identified by a variety of different properties. Listed here are some of the most important properties for a range of common rocks and minerals. Rocks are grouped here by their origin (where they formed), minerals by their chemical composition. Sometimes, a single property can identify a specimen; more often, a combination of properties is needed. Basalt rock, for example, is classified as a basic, extrusive igneous rock and identified by its dark colour and fine grain.

properties

ROCKS

NAME	ORIGIN	GRAIN SIZE	CLASSIFICATION	WHERE FORMED	COLOUR
IGNEOUS					
Granite	Intrusive	Coarse	Acid	Pluton	Light, Medium
Diorite	Intrusive	Coarse	Intermediate	Pluton, Dyke	Medium, Dark
Syenite	Intrusive	Coarse	Intermediate	Pluton, Dyke	Light, Dark
Gabbro	Intrusive	Coarse	Basic	Pluton	Medium
Dolerite	Intrusive	Medium	Basic	Dyke, Sill	Dark
Rhyolite	Extrusive	Fine	Acid	Volcano	Light
Obsidian	Extrusive	Very Fine	Acid	Volcano	Dark
Peridotite	Intrusive	Coarse	Ultrabasic	Pluton, Dyke, Sill	Dark
Andesite	Extrusive	Fine	Intermediate	Volcano	Medium
Basalt	Extrusive	Fine	Basic	Volcano	Dark
Tuff	Pyroclastic	Fine	Acid to basic	Volcano	Medium
Pumice	Extrusive	Fine	Acid to basic	Volcano	Medium

NAME	ORIGIN	GRAIN SIZE	CLASSIFICATION	PRESSURE	TEMPERATURE	STRUCTURE
METAMORPHIC						
Slate	Mountain ranges	Fine	Regional	Low	Low	Foliated
Schist	Mountain ranges	Medium	Regional	Moderate	Low to Moderate	Foliated
Gneiss	Mountain ranges	Coarse	Regional	High	High	Foliated, Crystalline
Amphibolite	Mountain ranges	Coarse	Regional	High	High	Foliated, Crystalline
Marble	Contact aureoles	Fine, Coarse	Contact	Low	High	Crystalline
Hornfels	Contact aureoles	Fine	Contact	Low to High	High	Crystalline
Metaquartzite	Contact aureoles	Medium	Contact	Low	High	Crystalline

NAME	ORIGIN	GRAIN SIZE	CLASSIFICATION	FOSSILS	GRAIN SHAPE
SEDIMENTARY					
Conglomerate	Marine, Freshwater	Very coarse	Clastic	Very rare	Rounded
Sandstone	Marine, Freshwater, Continental	Medium	Clastic	Invertebrates, Vertebrates, Plants	Angular, Rounded
Shale	Marine, Freshwater	Fine	Clastic	Invertebrates, Vertebrates, Plants	Angular
Mudstone	Marine, Freshwater	Fine	Clastic	Invertebrates, Plants	Angular
Clay	Marine, Freshwater, Continental	Fine	Clastic	Invertebrates, Vertebrates, Plants	Angular
Limestone	Marine	Medium, Coarse	Chemical	Invertebrates	Rounded
Chalk	Marine	Fine	Organic	Invertebrates, Vertebrates	Rounded, Angular
Dolomite	Marine	Medium, Fine	Chemical	Invertebrates	Crystalline
Travertine	Continental	Crystalline	Chemical	Rare	Crystalline
Anthracite	Continental	Medium, Fine	Organic	Plants	Amorphous

MINERALS

NAME	CHEMICAL FORMULA	HARDNESS	SPECIFIC GRAVITY	CLEAVAGE	FRACTURE
NATIVE ELEMENTS					
Gold	Au	$2_{1/2}$–3	19.3	None	Hackly (with rough edges)
Silver	Ag	$2_{1/2}$–3	10.5	None	Hackly
Copper	Cu	$2_{1/2}$–3	8.9	None	Hackly
Sulphur	S	$1_{1/2}$–$2_{1/2}$	2.0–2.1	Imperfect basal	Uneven to conchoidal
Diamond	C	10	3.52	Perfect octahedral	Conchoidal
Graphite	C	1–2	2.1–2.3	Perfect basal	Uneven
SULPHIDES					
Galena	PbS	$2_{1/2}$	7.58	Perfect cubic	Subconchoidal
Pyrite	FeS_2	6–$6_{1/2}$	5.0	Indistinct	Conchoidal to uneven
SULPHATES					
Gypsum	$CaSO_4.2H_2O$	2	2.32	Perfect	Splintery
Barite	$BaSO_4$	3–$3_{1/2}$	4.5	Perfect	Uneven
Wolframite	$(Fe,Mn)WO_4$	4–$4_{1/2}$	7.1–7.5	Perfect	Uneven
HALIDES					
Halite	$NaCl$	2	2.1–2.2	Perfect cubic	Uneven to conchoidal
Fluorite	CaF_2	4	3.18	Perfect octahedral	Conchoidal
OXIDES					
Spinel	$MgAl_2O_4$	$7_{1/2}$–8	3.5–4.1	None	Conchoidal to uneven
Hematite	Fe_2O_3	5–6	5.26	None	Uneven to subconchoidal
Corundum	Al_2O_3	9	4.0–4.1	None	Conchoidal to uneven
Perovskite	$CaTiO_3$	$5_{1/2}$	4.01	Imperfect	Subconchoidal to uneven
CARBONATES, NITRATES, AND BORATES					
Calcite	$CaCO_3$	3	2.71	Perfect	Subconchoidal
Malachite	$Cu_2CO_3(OH)_2$	$3_{1/2}$–4	4.0	Perfect	Subconchoidal to uneven
Nitratine	$NaNO_3$	$1_{1/2}$–2	2.27	Perf. rhombohedral	Conchoidal
Ulexite	$NaCaB_5O_6(OH)_6.5H_2O$	$2_{1/2}$	1.96	Perfect	Uneven
PHOSPHATES					
Turquoise	$CuAl_6(PO_4)_4(OH)_8.4H_2O$	5–6	2.6–2.8	Good	Conchoidal
Apatite	$Ca_5(PO_4)_3(F,Cl,OH)$	5	3.1–3.2	Poor	Conchoidal to uneven
SILICATES					
Quartz	SiO_2	7	2.65	None	Conchoidal to uneven
Opal	$SiO_2.nH_2O$	$5_{1/2}$–$6_{1/2}$	1.9–2.3	None	Conchoidal
Olivine	Fe_2SiO_4–Mg_2SiO_4	$6_{1/2}$–7	3.27–4.32	Imperfect	Conchoidal
Garnet	$Mg_3Al_2(SiO_4)_3$	$6_{1/2}$–$7_{1/2}$	3.4–4.3	None	Uneven to conchoidal
Beryl	$Be_3Al_2Si_6O_{18}$	7–8	2.6–2.9	Indistinct	Uneven to conchoidal
Hornblende	$Ca_2(Mg,Fe)_4Al(Si_7Al)O_{22}(OH,F)_2$	5–6	3–3.41	Perfect	Uneven
Diopside	$CaMgSi_2O_6$	$5_{1/2}$–$6_{1/2}$	3.22–3.38	Good	Uneven
Muscovite	$KAl_2(Si_3Al)O_{10}(OH,F)_2$	$2_{1/2}$–3	2.77–2.88	Perfect basal	Uneven
Kaolinite	$Al_2Si_2O_5(OH)_4$	2–$2_{1/2}$	2.6–2.63	Perfect basal	Uneven
Orthoclase	$KAlSi_3O_8$	6–$6_{1/2}$	2.55–2.63	Perfect	Uneven to conchoidal
ORGANIC					
Amber	Mixture of organic plant resins	$2_{1/2}$	1.08	None	Conchoidal

GLOSSARY

Abrasion The process of grinding or rubbing away a surface, such as a rock.

Acid Relating to rock with a high silica content.

Alloy A combination of two or more metals. Commonly used alloys include bronze (copper and tin) and stainless steel (iron and chromium).

Amygdale A hole in lava or pyroclastic rock containing minerals, such as calcite or quartz.

Asteroid A chunk of rock smaller than a planet, which orbits the Sun.

Asthenosphere The hot, partially molten layer of rock in the Earth's upper mantle, just below the lithosphere.

Atmosphere The layers of gases surrounding the Earth or another planet.

Basic Relating to rock with low silica content.

Batholith A vast igneous intrusion in the crust of more than 100 sq km (39 sq miles).

Bed A thin layer of sedimentary rock.

Bedding plane The boundary between beds of sedimentary rock that formed at different times.

Bedrock Solid rock that lies beneath loose deposits of soil and other matter.

Canyon A deep, steep-sided valley, typically cut by a river.

Cement A material that hardens on drying to bind particles together in sedimentary rock. Cement is also a material used for building, made from crushed lime and clay.

Cementation The stage in lithification when cement glues the sediment particles together.

Chondrite A stony meteorite containing tiny granules of pyroxene and olivine. These rocks are among the oldest objects ever found.

Clastic sediment Rock and mineral particles formed from eroded fragments of broken rock.

Cleavage The way a mineral or rock breaks in a certain plane (direction).

Compaction The stage in lithification when water and air is squeezed out of the buried sediments by the weight of overlying deposits.

Contact aureole The area around a large igneous intrusion where the rock has been altered by the heat of the magma.

Continental drift The slow movement of the Earth's continents on its surface.

Core The Earth's hot, dense iron-rich centre – liquid on the outside and solid at the centre.

Country rock The rock that surrounds a mineral deposit or igneous intrusion.

Crust The Earth's rigid outermost layer. It is divided into thicker, older continental crust (mainly granite) and thinner, more recent oceanic crust (mainly basalt).

Crystal A solid substance with a regular form and symmetrical faces. Crystals grow in many ways, such as when molten material cools, or when a solution containing a dissolved mineral evaporates. Large crystals grow very slowly.

Delta A fan-shaped area of sediment deposited where a river slows down and splits into many channels, before entering a lake or the sea.

Deposition The dropping of loose sediment carried by water, wind, or moving ice, when they slow down and lose their energy.

Dyke A thin, sheet-like igneous intrusion that cuts across older rock structures.

Element A substance, such as gold, that cannot be broken down into more simple substances.

Erosion The slow wearing away of rocks by moving water, ice, and wind.

Evaporite A natural salt or mineral left behind after the water it was dissolved in has dried up.

Extrusive igneous rock Rock that forms when lava from a volcano cools and solidifies.

Fault An extended fracture in rock along which rock masses move.

Felsic Relating to igneous rocks rich in feldspar and quartz minerals.

Flint A hard nodule of chert (a fine-grained quartz sedimentary rock) that forms in limestone. It fractures well and was used by Stone Age people to make knives and arrows.

Flood plain The flat area each side of a river that is covered in water when the river floods.

Fold Bends in rock strata (layers) caused by tectonic plate movement.

Foliation Banded patterns caused by the alignment of crystals within metamorphic rocks.

Fossil Mineralized impression or cast of ancient plant or animal.

Fossil fuel A fuel, such as coal, oil, and natural gas, which formed from decomposed plant matter buried deep beneath the ground.

Fracture The distinctive way a mineral breaks.

Gemstone A mineral, usually crystalline, such as diamond or ruby that is valued for its colour, sparkle, rarity, and hardness.

Geode A small rock cavity lined with crystals or other mineral matter.

Geologist Someone who studies the Earth.

Glacier A slowly moving mass of ice formed by the compaction of snow on mountains or near the Earth's poles.

Groundmass Compact, fine-grained mineral material in which larger crystals are embedded.

Habit The general shape of a mineral.

Hot spot Site of volcanic activity in the Earth's crust away from the plate boundaries, created by magma rising from the upper mantle.

Hydrothermal vein A crack in the rock through which very hot mineral waters circulate due to volcanic activity. As the waters cool, minerals start to crystallize, forming some of the Earth's most valuable gemstones and ores.

Ice Age A very cold period in the Earth's history, when vast ice sheets covered large parts of the world. The most recent glacial period, which lasted about 100,000 years and ended 12,000 years ago, affected much of North America and northern Europe.

Idiochromatic A mineral that is always the same colour because of its chemical composition. A mineral (such as quartz) that changes colour is known as allochromatic.

Igneous rock Rock formed as magma cools and hardens in the Earth's crust.

Inclusion A tiny crystal or mineral fragment embedded in another mineral.

Intrusive igneous rock Igneous rock that forms beneath the Earth's surface.

Joint A crack in the rock, usually vertical, caused by tiny movements in the rock due to shrinking and expansion.

Karst landscape A limestone landscape, full of dramatically eroded cliffs, gorges, and caves.

Lava Magma that has flowed onto the Earth's surface through a volcanic opening.

Lithification The process of turning loose sediments into rock through compacting and cementing them together over milllions of years.

Lithosphere The hard, topmost layer of the Earth. It is made up of the crust and the upper part of the mantle.

Loess Large deposits of uncemented, fine, wind-blown sediment.

Lustre The way in which light reflects off the surface of a mineral.

Mafic Relating to silicate minerals, rich in magnesium and iron, typically formed in basalt and other basic or ultramafic rocks.

Magma Molten rock beneath the Earth's crust that forms as parts of the mantle melt.

Magma chamber Underground reservoir of magma. It can erupt onto the Earth's surface as lava or harden to form a pluton.

Magnetosphere Magnetic forcefield in and around the Earth, created by the movement of iron in the core. It protects the Earth against charged particles streaming from the Sun.

Mantle The middle layer of the Earth, between the core and the crust. Geologists believe it consists of hot, dense rocks, such as peridotite.

Massive formation A mineral habit with no definite shape or crystal faces.

Matrix The fine mass of material in which larger crystals are set.

Metamorphic rock Rock formed when other rocks are transformed by heat and pressure.

Meteor Once a meteoroid (rock and dust debris in space) enters the Earth's atmosphere, it becomes a meteor or shooting star.

Meteorite A meteor that crashes onto the Earth's surface.

Mid-ocean ridge A long chain of undersea mountains that forms along the ocean bed where tectonic plates are moving apart.

Mineral A naturally occurring solid with certain regular characteristics, such as chemical composition and crystal shapes. Earth's rocks are made up of minerals.

Native element An element found naturally as a mineral in its pure form. It does not form part of a compound.

Nodule A hard, rounded, stony lump found in sedimentary rock, typically made from calcite, silica, pyrite, or gypsum.

Normal fault A fault in two blocks of rock, which are being pulled apart, allowing one of them to slip down.

Oolith Small, rounded grains that make up some sedimentary rocks.

Opaque Describes material that does not let light pass through it.

Ore A rock or mineral from which a metal can be extracted for a profit.

Organic Relating to living things.

Placer A deposit of sand or gravel in the bed of a river or lake, containing grains of valuable minerals, such as gold or diamonds.

Plate boundary Where tectonic plates meet in the Earth's crust. There are three types of plate boundary: convergent (where plates collide), divergent (where plates pull apart), and transform (where plates slide past each other).

Pluton Any body of intrusive igneous rock.

Porphyritic Igneous rock containing large, well-formed crystals mixed into a groundmass.

Precipitation Chemical process in which a substance is deposited in solid form from a solution.

Prism A solid geometric figure with a set of faces parallel to one of the axes. An axis is an imaginary line which divides something in half.

Pyroclastic Materials such as rock and ash thrown out by an explosive volcanic eruption.

Radioactivity The spontaneous emission of bursts of radiation (alpha, beta, or gamma rays) caused by the disintegration of the unstable atoms of certain elements, such as the metal uranium. Some radiation is harmful to people.

Refraction The bending of light rays as they pass through a transparent substance.

Regional metamorphism The creation of new metamorphic rocks over a wide area by heat and pressure, typically during mountain-building.

Rock Solid mixtures of minerals. There are three types: igneous, metamorphic, and sedimentary.

Sea-floor spreading The gradual widening of an ocean as new oceanic crust forms along the mid-ocean ridge.

Sediment Particles of rock, mineral, or organic matter that are carried by wind, water, and ice.

Sedimentary rock Rock formed from sediment that has been buried and squeezed solid by pressure from above.

Sill A thin, sheetlike, typically horizontal, igneous intrusion, inserted between rock layers.

Spar A crystalline, easily cleavable, translucent or transparent mineral.

Specific gravity Comparing a mineral's weight with the weight of an equal volume of water.

Speleothem A structure, such as a stalactite or stalagmite, formed in a cave by the precipitation of minerals from water.

Strike-slip fault A fault in which blocks of rock slide sideways past each other. A very large strike-slip fault occurring on the boundary of two tectonic plates is known as a transform fault.

Stromatolite Layered mounds of sediment formed by colonies of ancient types of bacteria.

Symmetry When two forms mirror each other on opposite sides of an imaginary dividing line.

Tectonic plate One of about 20 huge, floating rock slabs that make up the Earth's lithosphere.

Thrust fault A fault in which one block is thrust up and over another. If the angle is steeper than 45°, it is a reverse fault.

Translucent A substance that lets light through, but breaks the light up so that you cannot see through it clearly.

Transportation The carrying of loose sediment by rivers, wind, waves, and ice.

Trench A deep trough in the ocean floor.

Twinning When two or more crystals of the same mineral grow together.

Ultrabasic Relating to igneous rock with less than 45 per cent silica.

Ultramafic Relating to igneous rock with no quartz and little or no feldspar, made mostly of minerals such as olivine and pyroxene.

Unconformity A noticeable break in a sequence of sedimentary rock layers, due to an interruption in the laying down of sediments.

Uplift When rock structures are raised upwards by the movement of tectonic plates. Sediments formed on the seabed may be uplifted to become mountains and plains.

Volcano The site of an eruption of lava and hot gases from within the Earth. Magma flows up a central passage and erupts as lava.

Weathering The slow breakdown of rock by prolonged exposure to the weather, including moisture, frost, and acidic rainwater.

INDEX

A page number in **bold** refers to the main entry for that subject.

A

a'a (lava) 23
acicular crystals 46
acid lakes 82
acid rock 27, 92
Acoma Pueblo (New Mexico) 57
actinolite 59
agate 45, 61, 76
   blue lace 61
alabaster 66
albite 59
alchemy 79
alloys 80, 81, 92
aluminium 81
Amazon 19
amazonite 56
amber 39, 91
American Gold Rush 55
amethyst 45, 48, 60, 75
ammonites 38, 39, 65
amphibole 59
amphibolite 90
amulets 13
amygdales 27, 92
Andes 17, 30
andesite 25, 90
angelite 66
anhydrite 66
animals 40, 86
anorthite 58
anorthoclase 56
anorthosite 58
anthracite 41, 90
antimony 50, 51
apatite 47, 71, 91
Apollo 16 58
aquamarine 49
aragonite 70
Arches National Park (Utah) 19
Argyle mine (Australia) 74
arsenic 50, 51, 73
arsenides 65
artefacts 12, 13, 26, 52, 54, 56, 62, 69, 71, 76, 78, 83
artificial gems 75
ash, volcanic 22, 23, 24
asthenosphere 15, 92
atacamite 68
augite 59
aurora borealis 15
avalanches 18
axinite 46
azurite 48

B

barite 46, 67, 91
basalt 20, 24, 25, 27, 61, 90
basalt pillars 25
basic rock 27, 92
batholiths 24, 25, 27, 28, 92
Batura Glacier (Pakistan) 19
bedding planes 33, 92
beryl 46, 57, 91
bioclastic rock 40
biogenic rock 40
biotite 57
bismuth 50, 51
bituminous coal 41
blast furnaces 79
blood cells 87
blowouts 19
Blue John 69
Boars Tusk (Wyoming) 56

bone formation 87
borates 71, 91
borax 83
boron 86
botryoidal clusters 51
botryoidal crystals 46
boulders 32
bournonite 65
breccia 33, 43
British Imperial State Crown 62
bronze 78
Bronze Age 78
building materials 53, 72, 77, 79, 82, **84–85**

C

calcite 34, 36, 37, 40, 44, 46, 47, 49, 70, 77, 82, 91
calcium 86, 87
California 11, 17, 27, 35
carbon 51
carbon dioxide 18
carbonate rock 34
carbonates 45, **70–71**, 91
carbonic acid 18
Carlsbad Caverns (New Mexico) 37
carnelian 44
Carrara marble 29
cassiterite 63
cave paintings 36
cave pearls 37
caves **36–37**
cement 82, 84, 92
cerussite 73
chalcanthite 67
chalcedony 60, 91
chalcocite 65
chalcosine 65
chalk 40, 82, 90
chemical composition 27
chemical elements 50
chemical erosion 35
chemical properties 46
chemical rock 32
chemical sediments **34–35**
chemical structures 51
chemistry 79
China clay 83
chondrite 42, 43
chromates 67
chromium 81, 86
chrondite 90
cinders 24
cinnabar 64
cirques 19
citrine 48
clarity (of minerals) 49
classes of minerals **44–45**
clay 32, 84, 85, 90
cleavage 47, 92
cliffs 17, 19, 20, 31, 36, 40
coal 8, 41
cobalt 86
cobbles 32
cockscomb 67
"cog wheel ore" 65
coins 53, 54, 73
Colima Volcano (Mexico) 88
collision of plates 15, 16, 30
collision zone 30
colour (of minerals) 48
compass, magnetized 62
composite minerals 10
composite volcano 22
conchoidal fracture 47
concrete 83
conglomerates 33, 90
continental drift 13, 16, 17, 92
Coober Pedy (Australia) 61

copper 10, 13, 52, 67, 78, 80, 84, 86, 91
coral 40
core (of Earth) 14, 15, 92
corrosion, chemical 18
corundum 47, 91
crocoite 67
cross-bedding 33
crust (of Earth) 14, 15, 24, 92
cryogenic magnetometer 89
crystal 46, 92
   acicular 46
   amethyst 45
   azurite 49
   botryoidal 46
   calcite 70
   cubic 46, 68
   dendritic 46
   galena 64
   garnet 29
   gold 54
   hexagonal 46
   Iceland spar 49
   malachite 48
   massive 46
   monoclinic 46, 50
   orthorhombic 46, 50
   prismatic 46, 67
   pyrite 55
   reniform 46
   tetragonal 46
   tourmaline 25, 45
   triclinic 46
   trigonal 46
crystal balls 13
crystal habit 46
crystalline 67
crystallography 89
cubic crystal 46
cubic zirconia 75
cutting of gemstones 74

D

daisy 66
dangerous minerals 73
David, Michelangelo's 29
decorative rocks and minerals 9, **76–77**
deltas 19, 92
dentritic crystals 46
deposition 18, 19, 21, 92
desert oases 37
desert rose 66
deserts 19
detrital rock 32
diamonds 47, 51, 74, 75, 91
dinosaurs 38, 39
diopside 91
diorite 27, 90
discordant intrusions 25
dogtooth spar 70
dolerite 26, 90
dolomite 90
dolomitic limestone 34
domestic minerals **84–85**
dunes 19, 60
dust clouds 20
dykes 24, 25, 92

E

early uses of minerals **72–73**
earthquakes 17
   detection of 12
Earth's structure **14–15**
eclogite 59
effusive volcano 23

copper 10, 13, 52, 67, 78, 80, 84, 86, 91
electronics 54, 61, 83
elements 92
   chemical 50
   metal **52–53**
   native **50–51**, 91
emeralds 57, 75
enargite 65
Epsom salts 67
epsomite 67
erosion 8, 12, **18–19**, 20, 35, 56, 92
erratics 21
Eurasian plate 16, 17
evaporite 35, 44, 92
extrusive igneous rock 24, 92

F

faults 17, 92
feldspar 11, 26, 31, 45, 56, 58
felsic silicates **56–57**
ferns, fossil 39
fertilizers 8, 69
fieldwork 88, 89
fine-grain lava 26
fissure eruption 22
flint 35, 92
flint arrowheads 72
flint tools 72
floodplains 19, 92
fluorescence 49
fluorite 47, 49, 69, 91
   banded 69
Fly Geyser (Nevada) 70
folding 31, 92
foliation 31, 92
"fool's gold" 55
forminifera shells 40
fossil fuels 40, 92
fossiliferous limestone 40
fossilized organisms 40
fossils **38–39**, 40, 92
frost-shattering 20

G

gabbro 27, 90
gabbro batholith 28
galena 47, 64, 91
garnet 44, 75, 91
Geiger counter 88
gem-cutter 74
gemstones 13, **74–75**, 92
geological map 12
geologist's equipment 89
geology **88–89**
   history of **12–13**
Giant's Causeway (Ireland) 25
glacial erosion 19
glaciers 18, 19, 20, 92
glass 85
glass production 83
gneiss 30, 31, 90
gold 8, 49, 52, **54–55**, 91
grain size (of lava and magma) 26
Grand Canyon (Arizona) 8
granite 11, 26, 27, 28, 77, 85, 90
granite batholiths 25
granite carvings 26
graphite 49, 51, 91
gravel 84
greasy lustre 49
Great Pyramids 9
Gros Morne (Newfoundland) 14
gryke 18
gypsum 47, 49, 66, 91
gypsum plaster 82

H

halides 45, **68–69**, 91
halite 46, 49, 68, 91
   blue 68
   hopper crystal 68
   orange 68
Hawaii 21, 22, 23, 24, 58
health 86, 87
hematite 48, 62, 91
hematite habit 46
hexagonal crystals 46
hills 18, 36
Himalayan mountains 17
hip replacements (titanium) 81
historic metals **78–79**
history of geology **12–13**
horizontal sill 25
hornblende 91
hornfels 28, 90
hot springs 10, 44, 50
Huang He (China) 19
hydrozincite habit 46

I

ice 18, 36
Ice Ages 19, 92
Iceland spar 49, 70
Ichthyosaurus 38
igneous rock 10, 11, 20, 21, **24–27**, 90, 92
Indo-Australian plate 17
industrial minerals **82–83**
Industrial Revolution 79
inorganic rock 32
intermediate rocks 27
intrusions 25
intrusive igneous rock 24, 25, 92
iron 8, 14, 15, 79, 86, 87
iron bridge, world's first 79
iron in construction work 79
iron-nickels (meteorites) 43
irons (meteorites) 43
ironworking 79

JK

jade 76
Japan 16, 20
jasper 76
jewellery 51, 53, 62, 74, 75
K-feldspar 56
kaolin 83
kaolinite 91
karst 35, 92

L

labradorite 59
landslides 17
lapis lazuli 54, 72
Lascaux (France) 36
lava 13, 20, 21, 22, 23, 24, 25, 26, 61, 92
lava caves 36
layers of sediment 32
lead 53, 64, 67, 73
"lead" in pencils 51
lepidocrocite 49
lepidolite 57
life-forms, rock from **40–41**
lignite 41, 71
limestone 18, 28, 29, 35, 40, 84, 90

limestone caverns 36, 37
limonite 48
limonite habit 46
lithosphere 14, 15, 93
loess 19, 33, 93
London Eye (steel alloys) 80
lustre 48, 49, 93

M

mafic silicates **58–59**
magma 14, 15, 16, 20, 21, 22, 23, 24, 25, 26, 27, 28, 29, 93
magma chamber 24, 93
magnesium 15, 86
magnetic field 15, 89
magnetic properties 62
magnetic rock 15
magnetite 62
malachite 48, 70, 91
Mammoth Caves (Kentucky) 36
manganese 86
manganite 46
mantle 14, 15, 16, 93
marble 28, 29, 77, 90
Mariana trench 17
Mars 42, 43
massive crystals 46
massive habit 62
Mauna Loa (Hawaii) 22
medium-grain magma 26
mercury 53, 64
metal elements **52–53**
metallic lustre 49
metals 10, 50
    in history **78–79**
    modern **80–81**
metalware 83
metamorphic rock 10, 11, 20, 21, **28–29**, 30, 90
metamorphism, regional **30–31**
metaquartzite 28, 90
Meteor Crater (Arizona) 42
meteorites 42, 43, 90, 93
mica 31, 57, 83
mica biotite 11
mica window 57
microcline 56
microfossils 40
mid-ocean ridge 21, 93
mineral-rich waters 87
mineral supplements 87
mineraloids 45
minerals **10–11**, 15, 93
    classes of **44–45**
    decorative **76–77**
    early uses of **72–73**
    essential for life **86–87**
    formation of 35
    in the home **84–85**
    in industry **82–83**
    properties of **46–49**, **90–91**
mining 8, 41, 50, 55, 57, 61, 68, 74, 81
modern metals **80–81**
modern technology 80, 81
Mohs's hardness scale 47
molten rock (lava) 24
molybdates 67
molybdenum 86
Mono Lake (California) 35
monoclinic crystals 46, 50
Moon 58
Mount Etna (Italy) 22, 23
Mount Pinatubo (Philippines) 23
Mount Rushmore (USA) 26
Mount St Helens (USA) 23
Mount Vesuvius (Italy) 23
mountains 11, 14, 15, 17, 18, 27, 28, 30, 34, 36, 58
mud deposits 19

mudflows 23
mudstone 28, 29, 31, 33, 90
muscovite 47, 57, 91
myths 13, 25

N

nailhead spar 70
NASA 42, 43
native elements **50–51**, 91, 93
native lead 53
native minerals 44
natural gas 41
Navajo sandstone 33
Nazca plate 17
nickel 14, 15, 86
nickel-iron 42, 53
nickel ore 53
nickel-silver 53
Nile 19
nitrates 71, 91
nitratine 71, 91
nodules 35, 93
non-metals 10, 50
normal fault 17
North American plate 16, 17
North Sea oil 41
Northern Lights 15
nuclear fuel rods 63
nuées ardentes 23
Nullabor Plain (Australia) 37
nutrient minerals **86–87**

O

obsidian rock 26, 90
ocean floor 21
oceans 14, 15, 16, 17
oil 8, 41, 84
    drilling for 41
oil traps 41
oligoclase 58
olivine 58, 91
Olympus Mons 43
onyx 76
oolith formation 34
oolitic limestone 34
opalescence 61
opals 47, 61, 75, 91
opaque minerals 49, 93
optical properties **48–49**
organic gemstones 75
organic minerals 91
organic rock 40, 41
ornamental stone 76, 77
orpiment 48, 65
orthoclase 47, 56, 91
orthoclase habit 46
orthorhombic crystals 46, 50
oxides 44, **62–63**, 91

P

Pacific plate 16, 17
pahoehoe (lava) 23
paint 85
pallasites 43
Pamukkale (Turkey) 44, 45
Pantheon (Rome) 82
parallel dykes 25
pearls 75
peat 41
pebbles 32
pegmatite 25, 26
peridot 58
peridotite 14, 27, 90

Petra (Jordan) 72, 73
Philippine plate 16
phosphates 45, 71, 91
phosphorus 86, 87
phyllite 30
pigments from minerals 72
pillow lava 21
pitchblende 63
plagioclase feldspar 58, 59
plains 18
planes (alloys) 81
plants 41, 86
plate boundaries 16, 17, 93
plate tectonics **16–17**
plates 16, 17, 30
platinum 53
Plinian eruptions 23
pollution 81
Pompeii (Italy) 23
porcelain 56, 83
porphyries 26
potassium 56, 86
potholes 36
pottery 72
power cables (aluminium) 81
precipitates 34
prismatic crystals 46, 67, 93
properties of minerals **46–49**, **90–91**
proustite 65
pumice 90
pyrite 35, 55, 65, 91
pyroclastic flows 23, 93
pyrolusite habit 46
pyroxene 14, 58, 59

QR

Qinghae Salt Lake (China) 35
quarrying 8, 29, 31
quartz 11, 13, 15, 28, 31, 47, 52, 57, **60–61**, 63, 75, 91
    milky 60
    rose 60
    rutilated 63
    smoky 60
quartzite 29
Queen Elizabeth I 73
radioactivity 88, 93
radium 63
realgar 65
refraction 49, 93
reniform crystals 46
reniform habit 62
reverse fault 17
rhodochrosite 70
rhyolite 26, 90
rift valley 15
ring dykes 25
"Ring of Fire" 22
rivers 19
rock **10–11**, 93
    properties of **90–91**
rock crystal (quartz) 60
rock cycle **20–21**
rock debris 18, 19
rock formation 24
rock salt 68
rubellite 57
rubies 49, 63
"ruby silver" 65
rutile 63

S

Sahara 19, 60
salt 8, 35, 68
salt consumption 73, 86

salt lakes 35
salt mountains 68
San Andreas fault 17
sand 19, 32, 58, 60, 84
sandstone 28, 29, 31, 33, 72, 90
sanidine 56
sapphires 62, 63, 75
sardonyx 76
satellite technology 88
satin spar 66
schist 29, 30, 44, 90
scree 11
sculpture 26, 29, 66, 72, 77
sea caves 36
sea salt 68
sedimentary rock 10, 11, 20, 21, 24, **32–33**, 35, 38, 40, 90, 93
selenium 86
semi-metals 50, 51
septarian nodule 35
Serapis, Pillars of 13
shale 90
shellfish (fossils) 38, 39
shield volcano 22
shooting stars 42
Sierra Nevada (California) 11, 27
silica 83, 84, 85
silicates 44, 60, 91
    felsic **56–57**
    mafic **58–59**
silicon 15
silicon chips 61
silky lustre 49
sillimanite 47
sills 24, 25, 93
silt 19, 32
Silurian limestone 40
silver 52, 91
sinkholes 36, 37
slate 30, 31, 90
smelting 78
sodium 86
Solar System 42, 43, 58
solecite habit 46
solution caves 36
South American plate 17
space rock **42–43**
space shuttle 9
spar 93
specific gravity 47, 93
specularite habit 62
sphene 59
spinel 62, 91
"spotted" rock 28
stalactite 36, 37, 45
stalagmite 37
staurolite 59
steel 8, 79, 84
steel alloys 80
steel production 80
steelmaking 69
Stone Age 8
stones (meteorites) 43
stony irons (meteorites) 43
stratovolcano 22
streak test 48
strike-slip fault 17, 93
stromatolites 89, 93
Strombolian eruption 22
subducted plates 20, 30
subduction 15
submetallic lustre 49
sulphates 44, **66–67**, 91
sulphides 44, **64–65**, 91
sulphosalts 65
sulphur 10, 50, 86, 91
sulphuric acid 50
sunscreen (zinc) 81
Super Pit (Australia) 8
syenite 90
sylvanite 65
sylvite 69

T

Taj Mahal (India) 9
talc 47, 83
tarnishing 52
tectonic plates **16–17**, 20, 22, 28, 30, 88, 93
tektite 42
tellurides 65
"Terracotta Army" 72
tetragonal crystals 46
Thingvellir (Iceland) 16
thrust fault 17, 93
tin 63
titanite 59
titanium 63, 81
titanium dioxide 85
tooth fillings (mercury) 53
topaz 47, 75
tourmaline 25, 45, 75
trace fossils 38
transform fault 17, 93
translucent minerals 49
transparent minerals 49
travertine 90
travertine calcite 70
trench 17, 93
triclinic crystals 46
trigonal crystals 46
tufa 35
tuff 24, 90
tungstates 67
tungsten 67
turquoise 71, 91
Tutankhamun's funeral mask 54
Twelve Apostles (Australia) 19
twinning 59, 93
Tyrannosaurus rex 39

UV

U-shaped valleys 19
ulexite 71, 91
ultrabasic rocks 27, 93
unconformity 33, 93
underground lakes 36
underwater geology 89
uneven fracture 47
uraninite 63
uranium 63
valleys 18
vertical dyke 25
vesuvianite 46
vitamins 86, 87
vitreous lustre 49
volcanic plug 25, 56
volcanoes 8, 13, 14, 15, 20, **22–23**, 24, 43, 64, 88, 93
vulcanology 8

WYZ

water 18
water erosion 19
wavellite 71
waves 19
weathering 18, 20, 93
White Cliffs of Dover 40
wind 18
wind erosion 19
wolframite 67, 91
wulfenite 67
Yellowstone Park (Wyoming) 10
Yosemite (California) 27
Yunshui Caverns (China) 37
zeolite 27
zinc 81, 86

ACKNOWLEDGEMENTS

Dorling Kindersley would like to thank Marion Dent for proof-reading; Michael Dent for the index; Margaret Parrish for Americanization; Judith Samuelson and Andrew Kerr-Jarrett for editorial support; and Leah Germann for design support.

Dorling Kindersley Ltd is not responsible and does not accept liability for the availability or content of any web site other than its own, or for any exposure to offensive, harmful, or inaccurate material that may appear on the Internet. Dorling Kindersley Ltd will have no liability for any damage or loss caused by viruses that may be downloaded as a result of looking at and browsing the web sites that it recommends. Dorling Kindersley downloadable images are the sole copyright of Dorling Kindersley Ltd, and may not be reproduced, stored, or transmitted in any form or by any means for any commercial or profit-related purpose without prior written permission of the copyright owner.

Picture Credits
The publisher would like to thank the following for their kind permission to reproduce their photographs:

Abbreviations key:
t-top, b-bottom, r-right, l-left, c-centre, a-above, f-far

8: Corbis/R.L.Christiansen (l), Reuters/Will Burgess (br); 8–9: Corbis/Liz Hymans (t); 9: Corbis (r), Georgina Bowater (cl), Peter Guttman (detail, c), Sally A.Morgan/Ecoscene (b); 10: Corbis/Layne Kennedy (l); 11: GeoScience Features Picture Library (tc), FLPA/Minden Pictures (r); 12: Lonely Planet Images/Andrew MacColl (bc), British Geological Survey (br); 13: www.bridgeman.co.uk/Chartres Cathedral, France (bc); Corbis/Jonathan Blair (tl), Sandro Vannini (br), Werner Forman Archive/University of Philadelphia Museum (bcl); 14: Corbis/Raymond Gehman (acr), Science Photo Library/Alfred Pasieka (fbcl), Dirk Wiersma (acl, bcl), Stephen & Donna O'Meara (bl); 15: Corbis/Bjorn Backe/Papilio (t); 16: Science Photo Library/Bernhard Edmaier (br), Tom Van Sant/Planetary Visions/Geosphere Project (tr); 17: Ardea.com/Francois Gohier (bl), Corbis (tr), GeoScience Features Picture Library (crb, bcr), Marli Miller/Department of Geological Sciences, University of Oregon (fbcr), Science Photo Library/Geospace (tl); 18: Corbis/O. Alamany & E.Vicens (bcl), Roger Antrobus (bl); 18–19: Impact Photos/Pamla Toler (t), Corbis/Jonathan Blair (c), W. Wayne Lockwood, M.D. (b); 19: Ardea/Alan Weaving (tr), Corbis (bcr), Phil Schermeister (br), Yann Arthus-Bertrand (acr); 20: Corbis/Homer Sykes (tr), Science Photo Library/2002 Orbital Imaging Corporation (acl); 21: Ardea/Jean-Paul Ferrero (tl), Bryan Sage (tc), Corbis/David Muench (c), Corbis/Digital image © 1996, courtesy of NASA (tcl), Gary Braasch (tcr), GeoScience Features Picture Library (tr), Science Photo Library/B.Murton, Southampton Oceanography Centre (bcr); 22: Corbis/Reuters (l); 23: Natural Visions/Soames Summerhays (acr), Corbis/Alberto Garcia (bl), Corbis/Digital image © 1996, courtesy of NASA (cr), Roger Ressmeyer (tl, tr), FLPA/USDA (cl);

24: Corbis/Roger Ressmeyer (r); 25: Corbis/Ric Ergenbright (t), Galen Rowell (cl); Geoscience Features Picture Library/RIDA (bcl), Marli Miller/Dept of Geological Sciences, University of Oregon (fbcl); 26: The Art Archive/Staatliche Sammlung Ägyptischer Kunst Munich/Dagli Orti (c); 26–27: Corbis/Joseph Sohm/Visions of America (b), 27: Corbis/David Muench (tr); 28: Corbis: Galen Rowell (r), GeoScience Features Picture Library (acl); 29: Corbis/Detail of David by Michelangelo/Arte & Immagini srl (br), Wild Country (bl); 30: Corbis/Hubert Stadler (b); 31: Corbis/Steve Austin/Papilio (tr), Richard Klune (cl), Sean Sexton Collection (cr), FLPA/Ken Day (br); 32: FLPA/Christiana Carvalho (l); 33: Science Photo Library/Martin Bond (tl), Ardea.com/Francois Gohier (tr); 34: Corbis/Digital image © 1996, courtesy of NASA (tr), M. L. Sinibaldi (br), GeoScience Features Picture Library (c); 35: FLPA/Mark Newman (r), Natural Visions (cr, br); 36: Corbis/Gianni Dagli Orti (br); 36–37: Getty Images/The Image Bank (t); 37 Ardea.com/Jean-Paul Ferrero (br). Ian Beames (bcr), Bruce Coleman Ltd/Jules Cowan (tr, acr), Corbis/Sharna Balfour/Gallo Images (bl); 38: Ardea.com/Francois Gohier (acr), Corbis/Jonathan Blair (b); 39: Natural Visions (tl), Ardea.com/Francois Gohier (bcl, bcr), John Cancalosi (tc); 40: Natural Visions/Heather Angel (acr), Ardea.com/Kurt Amsler (br), Corbis/Bob Krist (tl), Science Photo Library/Andrew Syred (bl); 41: Corbis/Michael St. Maur Sheil (br), Roger Ressmeyer (acr); 42: Robert Visser (acr); GeoScience Features Picture Library (cl, c); 42–43: Science Photo Library/Jerry Lodriguss (t), Corbis/Charles & Josette Lenars (b); 43: Corbis/NASA/JPL/Cornell/Zuma (bcr), Science Photo Library/David Parker (tl), Nasa/US Geological Survey (tr); 44–45: Corbis/Christine Osborne (t); 47: Science Photo Library/Manfred Kage (br); 50: Corbis/Ludovic Maisant (c), Science Photo Library/Simon Fraser (b); 51: Corbis/Michael Prince (tl), Tom Stewart (tr), Science Photo Library/Charles D. Winters (c), Chemical Design (cl); 52: Natural Visions/Heather Angel (cr), Ardea.com/E. Mickleburgh (bl), Royalty-Free/Corbis (bcl); 53: Corbis/Douglas Whyte (tc), Gleb Garanich (cl), Nik Wheeler (bcr), Science Photo Library/Charles D. Winters (br), Scott Camazine (tr); 54: Corbis/Mike Simons (bc), Sandro Vannini (l), Science Photo Library/Andrew Syred (br), Rosenfeld Images Ltd (bcl); 55: Corbis/Bettmann (tr), Paul A. Souders (br), Wayne Lawler/Ecoscene (cr); 56: Corbis/Jeff Vanuga (t), Royal Ontario Museum (bcr), Science Photo Library/Roberto de Gugliemo (bcl); 57: Corbis/Lowell Georgia (tl), Reuters (br); 58: Corbis/James L. Amos (bl), Neil Rabinowitz (cl), NASA (br); 60: Corbis/Sergio Pitamitz (b); 61: Corbis/Dave G. Houser (br); 62: Corbis/Tim Graham (tl); 63: Corbis/Koopman (cl), Ron Watts (cr), Roger Ressmeyer (bl); 64: Corbis/Sandro Vannini (l); 64–65 Geophotos/Tony Waltham (b); 66: British Museum/Dorling Kindersley (tl), Corbis/Angelo Hornak (b), Maurice Nimmo/Frank Lane Picture Agency (cr), GeoScience Features Picture Library (acl); 67: Corbis/Owen Franken (acr); 68: Corbis/Kevin Shafer (t), Impact Photos/Alain Evrard (cr), Science Photo Library/David Nunuk (bc); 69: © Christie's Images Ltd (tc), Corbis/Richard Hamilton Smith (br), William Taufic (cl); 70: Science Photo Library/Arnold Fisher (cl), Keith Kent (acr); 71: INAH/Dorling Kindersley

(c), Science Photo Library/Biophoto Associates (cl), Lawrence Lawry (br), Sidney Moulds (bl); 72: Alamy Images/Keren Su/China Span (bl), Corbis/Francis G. Mayer (cr), Jose Manuel Sanchis Calvete (cl), Maurice Nimmo/Frank Lane Picture Agency (t); 73: www.bridgeman.co.uk/Osterreichische Nationalbibliothek, Vienna, Austria (br), Leeds Museums and Art Galleries (Temple Newsam House), UK (tr), Corbis/Archivo Iconografico, S.A (tl), Richard T. Nowitz (bl); 74: © Christie's Images Ltd (tr), Corbis/Jack Fields (br), Reuters (bcl), Roger Garwood & Trish Ainslie (fcl); 75: The Art Archive/Central Bank Teheran/Dagli Orti (tl), Judith Miller/Dorling Kindersley/Fellow & Sons (acl), V & A Images/Victoria and Albert Museum (bcl); 76: www.bridgeman.co.uk/Hermitage, St Petersburg, Russia (tr, fcr), Oriental Museum, Durham University, UK (cl); 76–77: Corbis/Asian Art & Archaeology, Inc (b); 77: Construction Photography.com/Adrian Sherratt (bcl), Corbis/Hans Georg Roth (ac), The Art Archive/Acropolis Museum Athens/Dagli Orti (r), Impact Photos/Alan Keohane (l); 78: Werner Forman Archive/British Museum (t), Akg-images/Erich Lessing (cr), Corbis/Bettmann (bl), Werner Forman (cl); 79: Akg-images/British Library (tr), Corbis/David Cumming/Eye Ubiquitous (tc), Hulton-Deutsch Collection (tl), Robert Estall (bl), Stapleton Collection (cr); 80: Corbis/Alex Steedman (l), Paul A. Souders (r); 81: Action Plus/Glyn Kirk (tr), Corbis (bcr), Charles E. Rotkin (bl), Guy Motil (tc), James L. Amos (cl), Photomorgana (tl); 82: Corbis/Bill Ross (l), Macduff Everton (cr), Ted Spiegel (br), ImageState/Pictor/StockImage (bl); 83: Judith Miller/Dorling Kindersley/Sloans & Kenyon (tc), Corbis/Charles E. Rotkin (cl), Christina Louiso (bcl), Jan Butchofsky-Houser (bc), Morton Beebe (r), Michael and Patricia Fogden (tl); 84: Construction Photography.com/Chris Henderson (br), Royalty-Free/Imagestate (bc), Royalty-Free/Getty Images/Photodisc Blue (bl); 85: Corbis/Brownie Harris (br), Edifice (tr), Royalty-Free/Corbis (cr, bl, bc); 86: Corbis/Peter Johnson (cr), OSF/photolibrary.com (cl), Science Photo Library/Microfield Scientific Ltd (tr); 87: Corbis/Layne Kennedy (bl), Royalty-Free/Corbis (br), Science Photo Library/Innerspace Imaging (tl), Insolite Realite (cl); 88: Corbis/Roger Ressmeyer (tr, br), Science Photo Library/Paolo Koch (cl); 89: Corbis/Jonathan Blair (tl), Layne Kennedy (cr), Science Photo Library/Geoff Lane/CSIRO (cl).

Jacket images
Front: Corbis: Joseph Sohm/ChromoSohm Inc. (crr); Science Photo Library: Lawrence Lawry (cr); Dirk Wiersma (cll). **Spine:** Corbis: Joseph Sohm/ChromoSohm Inc. (c). **Back:** Corbis: Jonathan Blair (cll); Science Photo Library: John Walsh (cr); Dirk Wiersma (cl, crr).

All other images © Dorling Kindersley.
For further information see:
www.dkimages.com